The Elements of
Moral Philosophy

SIXTH EDITION

JAMES RACHELS

Sixth Edition by

STUART RACHELS

 Higher Education

Boston   Burr Ridge, IL   Dubuque, IA   New York   San Francisco   St. Louis
Bangkok   Bogotá   Caracas   Kuala Lumpur   Lisbon   London   Madrid   Mexico City
Milan   Montreal   New Delhi   Santiago   Seoul   Singapore   Sydney   Taipei   Toronto

Higher Education

Published by McGraw-Hill, an imprint of The McGraw-Hill Companies, Inc., 1221 Avenue of the Americas, New York, NY 10020. Copyright © 2010, 2007, 2003, 1999, 1993, 1986. All rights reserved. No part of this publication may be reproduced or distributed in any form or by any means, or stored in a database or retrieval system, without the prior written consent of The McGraw-Hill Companies, Inc., including, but not limited to, in any network or other electronic storage or transmission, or broadcast for distance learning.

This book is printed on acid-free paper.

1 2 3 4 5 6 7 8 9 0 DOC/DOC 0 9

ISBN: 978-0-07-338671-3
MHID: 0-07-338671-5

Editor in Chief: *Michael Ryan*
Editorial Director: *Beth Mejia*
Sponsoring Editor: *Mark Georgiev*
Marketing Manager: *Pamela Cooper*
Managing Editor: *Nicole Bridge*
Production Editor: *David Blatty*
Design Manager: *Margarite Reynolds*
Production Supervisor: *Louis Swaim*
Composition: *11/12 Baskerville by Laserwords*
Printing: *R. R. Donnelley & Sons*

Cover art: Aleksandr Rodchenko. (1891–1956). Non-Objective Painting no. 80 (Black on Black), 1918. Oil on canvas, 32 1/4 × 31 1/4". Gift of the Artist, through Jay Leyda. (114. 1936). Digital Image © The Museum of Modern Art/Licensed by Scala/Art Resource, NY. © Aleksandr Rodchenko/RAO, Moscow/VAGA, New York.

Library of Congress Cataloging-in-Publication Data

Rachels, James, 1941–2003.
    The elements of moral philosophy. — 6th ed. / James Rachels, Stuart Rachels.
        p. cm.
    Includes bibliographical references (p. 184) and index.
    ISBN-13: 978-0-07-338671-3 (alk. paper)
    ISBN-10: 0-07-338671-5 (alk. paper)
    1. Ethics—Textbooks. I. Rachels, Stuart, 1969- II. Title.
    BJ1012.R29 2010
    170—dc22   2009000733

The Internet addresses listed in the text were accurate at the time of publication. The inclusion of a Web site does not indicate an endorsement by the authors or McGraw-Hill, and McGraw-Hill does not guarantee the accuracy of the information presented at these sites.

www.mhhe.com

About the Authors

JAMES RACHELS (1941–2003) wrote *The End of Life: Euthanasia and Morality* (1986), *Created from Animals: The Moral Implications of Darwinism* (1990), *Can Ethics Provide Answers? And Other Essays in Moral Philosophy* (1997), *Problems from Philosophy* (first edition, 2005), and *The Legacy of Socrates: Essays in Moral Philosophy* (2007). His website is www.jamesrachels.org.

STUART RACHELS is Associate Professor of Philosophy at the University of Alabama. He has revised several of James Rachels' books, including *Problems from Philosophy* (second edition, 2009) and *The Right Thing to Do* (fifth edition, 2010), which is the companion anthology to this book. Stuart won the United States Chess Championship in 1989, at the age of 20, and he is a Bronze Life Master at bridge. His website is www.jamesrachels.org/stuart.

Contents

Preface   ix
About the Sixth Edition   xi

1. WHAT IS MORALITY?   1

1.1.   The Problem of Definition   1
1.2.   First Example: Baby Theresa   1
1.3.   Second Example: Jodie and Mary   5
1.4.   Third Example: Tracy Latimer   7
1.5.   Reason and Impartiality   10
1.6.   The Minimum Conception of Morality   13

2. THE CHALLENGE OF CULTURAL RELATIVISM   14

2.1.   Different Cultures Have Different Moral Codes   14
2.2.   Cultural Relativism   16
2.3.   The Cultural Differences Argument   17
2.4.   What Follows from Cultural Relativism   19
2.5.   Why There Is Less Disagreement Than It Seems   21
2.6.   Some Values Are Shared by All Cultures   23
2.7.   Judging a Cultural Practice to Be Undesirable   24
2.8.   Back to the Five Claims   27
2.9.   What We Can Learn from Cultural Relativism   29

3. SUBJECTIVISM IN ETHICS   32

3.1. *The Basic Idea of Ethical Subjectivism*   *32*
3.2. *The Evolution of the Theory*   *33*
3.3. *The First Stage: Simple Subjectivism*   *34*
3.4. *The Second Stage: Emotivism*   *36*
3.5. *The Role of Reason in Ethics*   *39*
3.6. *Are There Proofs in Ethics?*   *41*
3.7. *The Question of Homosexuality*   *44*

4. DOES MORALITY DEPEND ON RELIGION?   48

4.1. *The Presumed Connection between Morality and Religion* *48*
4.2. *The Divine Command Theory*   *50*
4.3. *The Theory of Natural Law*   *53*
4.4. *Religion and Particular Moral Issues*   *57*

5. ETHICAL EGOISM   62

5.1. *Is There a Duty to Help Starving People?*   *62*
5.2. *Psychological Egoism*   *63*
5.3. *Three Arguments for Ethical Egoism*   *69*
5.4. *Three Arguments against Ethical Egoism*   *74*

6. THE IDEA OF A SOCIAL CONTRACT   80

6.1. *Hobbes's Argument*   *80*
6.2. *The Prisoner's Dilemma*   *83*
6.3. *Some Advantages of the Social Contract Theory* *87*
6.4. *The Problem of Civil Disobedience*   *90*
6.5. *Difficulties for the Theory*   *93*

7. THE UTILITARIAN APPROACH   97

7.1. *The Revolution in Ethics*   *97*
7.2. *First Example: Euthanasia*   *98*
7.3. *Second Example: Marijuana*   *101*
7.4   *Third Example: Nonhuman Animals*   *104*

8. THE DEBATE OVER UTILITARIANISM   109

8.1.	*The Classical Version of the Theory*	*109*
8.2.	*Is Pleasure All That Matters?*	*109*
8.3.	*Are Consequences All That Matter?*	*111*
8.4.	*Should We Be Equally Concerned for Everyone?*	*115*
8.5.	*The Defense of Utilitarianism*	*116*
8.6.	*Concluding Thoughts*	*122*

9. ARE THERE ABSOLUTE MORAL RULES?   124

9.1.	*Harry Truman and Elizabeth Anscombe*	*124*
9.2.	*The Categorical Imperative*	*127*
9.3.	*Kant's Arguments on Lying*	*129*
9.4.	*Conflicts between Rules*	*132*
9.5.	*Kant's Insight*	*133*

10. KANT AND RESPECT FOR PERSONS   136

10.1.	*Kant's Core Ideas*	*136*
10.2.	*Retribution and Utility in the Theory of Punishment*	*139*
10.3.	*Kant's Retributivism*	*141*

11. FEMINISM AND THE ETHICS OF CARE   146

11.1.	*Do Women and Men Think Differently about Ethics?*	*146*
11.2.	*Implications for Moral Judgment*	*152*
11.3.	*Implications for Ethical Theory*	*156*

12. THE ETHICS OF VIRTUE   158

12.1.	*The Ethics of Virtue and the Ethics of Right Action*	*158*
12.2.	*The Virtues*	*160*
12.3.	*Two Advantages of Virtue Theory*	*168*
12.4.	*Virtue and Conduct*	*169*
12.5.	*The Problem of Incompleteness*	*170*
12.6.	*Conclusion*	*172*

13. WHAT WOULD A SATISFACTORY MORAL THEORY BE LIKE?   173

13.1.	*Morality without Hubris*	*173*
13.2.	*Treating People as They Deserve*	*175*
13.3.	*A Variety of Motives*	*176*
13.4.	*Multiple-Strategies Utilitarianism*	*177*
13.5.	*The Moral Community*	*180*
13.6.	*Justice and Fairness*	*181*
13.7.	*Conclusion*	*183*

Notes on Sources   184
Index   195

Preface

Socrates, one of the first and best moral philosophers, said that morality is about "no small matter, but how we ought to live." This book is an introduction to moral philosophy, conceived in that broad sense.

In writing this book, I have been guided by the following thought: Suppose someone knows nothing about ethics but wants to learn about it. What are the first things he or she should know? This book is my answer to that question. I do not try to cover every topic in the field; I do not even provide a complete account of the topics I do cover. Instead, I try to discuss the most important ideas that a newcomer should confront.

The chapters have been written so that they may be read independently of one another—they are, in effect, separate essays. Thus someone who is interested in Ethical Egoism could go straight to Chapter 5 and find a self-contained introduction to that theory. When read in order, however, the chapters tell a more or less continuous story. The first presents a "minimum conception" of what morality is; the middle chapters cover the most important ethical theories; and the last chapter presents my own view of what a satisfactory moral theory would be like.

The point of this book is not to provide a neat, unified account of "the truth" about ethics. That would be a poor way to introduce the subject. Philosophy is not like physics. In physics, there is a large body of established truth that beginners must patiently master. (Physics teachers rarely invite their students to make up their own minds about the laws of thermodynamics.) There are, of course, unresolved controversies in physics, but these take place against the backdrop of broad agreement. In philosophy, by contrast, everything is controversial—or almost everything. Competent philosophers disagree even about fundamental matters. A good introduction will not try to hide that somewhat embarrassing fact.

You will find, then, a survey of contending ideas, theories, and arguments. My own views inevitably color the presentation. I find some of these ideas more appealing than others, and a philosopher who made different assessments would no doubt write a different book. But I do try to present the contending ideas fairly, and when I endorse or reject an argument, I try to explain why. Philosophy, like morality itself, is first and last an exercise in reason—the ideas that should prevail are the ones best supported by the arguments. If this book is success-ful, then the reader can begin to assess where the weight of reason rests.

About the Sixth Edition

Professor Heather Elliott and I read the fifth edition of this book aloud to one another, pausing to discuss each paragraph. Our discussions helped me to clarify arguments, fix organizational problems, and remove about 10,000 words from the text without loss of content. Here is a summary of some of the changes in the new edition:

- In Chapter 2, "The Challenge of Cultural Relativism," I reversed the order of the final two sections, and I added a brief discussion of polyamory (section 2.9).
- In Chapter 3, "Subjectivism in Ethics," I expanded the discussion of "family values" (section 3.7).
- In Chapter 4, "Does Morality Depend on Religion?" I added a third reason to reject Natural Law Theory (section 4.3), and I now cite additional pro-choice passages in the Bible (section 4.4).
- In Chapter 5, "Ethical Egoism," I added two amazing examples of altruism by Oseola McCarty and Wesley Autrey (section 5.2), and I eliminated the argument that Ethical Egoism cannot handle conflicts of interest (section 5.4). Section 5.4 is still called "*Three* Arguments against Ethical Egoism" because the argument about wicked actions now gets its own billing.
- In Chapter 6, "The Idea of a Social Contract," I changed the terminology in the Prisoner's Dilemma from "acting egoistically" to "acting selfishly" (section 6.2); I improved the discussion of the theory's second and fourth advantages (section 6.3); I added examples of civil disobedience (section 6.4); and I revised the section on objections (6.5). This chapter now follows "Ethical Egoism" in recognition of the contract theory's egoistic roots.

- In Chapter 7, "The Utilitarian Approach," I replaced the Matthew Donnelly example—which turned out to be fictitious—with the story of how Sigmund Freud died (section 7.2). I also added a section on marijuana (7.3) and updated the discussion of vivisection (section 7.4).
- In Chapter 8, "The Debate over Utilitarianism," I revised the treatment of Rule Utilitarianism (section 8.5).
- In Chapter 9, "Are There Absolute Moral Rules?" I now note a limitation to the "Conflicts between Rules" argument (section 9.4).
- In Chapter 10, "Kant and Respect for Persons," I rewrote the opening section; I corrected the discussion of rehabilitation in American prisons (section 10.2); and I now mention both "turning the other cheek" and the possibility of wrongful execution (section 10.3).
- In Chapter 11, "Feminism and the Ethics of Care," I added empirical data to the discussion of how women and men think (section 11.1).
- In Chapter 12, "The Ethics of Virtue," I revised the section arguing that radical virtue ethics is incomplete (section 12.5).

I describe the changes to this book in greater detail on my website: www.jamesrachels.org/stuart.

For their help, I thank Robert Agnew, Aysha Akhtar, Colin Allen, Torin Alter, Luke Barber, Lance Basting, Saul Brenner, Nicole Bridge, Dave Bzdak, Michael Cholbi, Edgar Dahl, Kyle Driggers, Kym Farrand, Talia Finkelstein, Daniel Hollingshead, Mike Huemer, Larry James, Kevin Kukla, Carlo Maley, Christina Matthies, Sean McAleer, Cayce Moore, Nathan Nobis, Michael Patton, Vida Pavesich, Howard Pospesel, Jesse Prinz, Roger Rigterink, Amy Robinson, Robert Veatch, and McGraw-Hill's outstanding anonymous reviewers. My biggest debts are to David Blatty, the gold standard of editors; my mother, Carol Rachels, who proofread and vetted each change; and my fiancée, Heather Elliott, whose brilliant mind improved the book on every page.

We all miss James Rachels, who was the sole author of this book in its first four editions. To learn more about him, visit www.jamesrachels.org.

Tell me your thoughts about the book: srachels@bama.ua.edu.

—Stuart Rachels

CHAPTER 1

What Is Morality?

We are discussing no small matter, but how we ought to live.
SOCRATES, IN PLATO'S *REPUBLIC* (ca. 390 B.C.)

1.1. The Problem of Definition

Moral philosophy is the effort to understand the nature of morality and what it requires of us—in Socrates' words, to understand "how we ought to live" and why. It would be helpful if we could begin with a simple, uncontroversial definition of what morality is, but that turns out to be impossible. There are many rival theories, each expounding a different conception of what it means to live morally, and any definition that goes beyond Socrates' simple formulation is bound to offend at least one of them.

This should make us cautious, but it need not paralyze us. In this chapter, I will describe the "minimum conception" of morality. As the name suggests, the minimum conception is a core that every moral theory should accept, at least as a starting point. First, however, we will examine some moral controversies having to do with handicapped children. The features of the minimum conception will emerge from our discussion.

1.2. First Example: Baby Theresa

Theresa Ann Campo Pearson, an infant known to the public as "Baby Theresa," was born in Florida in 1992. Baby Theresa had anencephaly, one of the worst genetic disorders. Anencephalic infants are sometimes referred to as "babies without brains," and this gives roughly the right picture, but it is not quite accurate.

1

Important parts of the brain—the cerebrum and cerebellum—are missing, as is the top of the skull. There is, however, a brain stem, and so autonomic functions such as breathing and heartbeat are possible. In the United States, most cases of anencephaly are detected during pregnancy, and the fetuses are usually aborted. Of those not aborted, half are stillborn. About 350 are born alive each year, and they usually die within days.

Baby Theresa's story is remarkable only because her parents made an unusual request. Knowing that their baby would die soon and could never be conscious, Theresa's parents volunteered her organs for transplant. They thought her kidneys, liver, heart, lungs, and eyes should go to other children who could benefit from them. Her physicians agreed. Thousands of infants need transplants each year, and there are never enough organs available. But the organs were not taken, because Florida law forbids the removal of organs until the donor is dead. By the time Baby Theresa died, nine days later, it was too late for the other children—her organs had deteriorated too much to be harvested and transplanted.

Baby Theresa's case was widely debated. Should she have been killed so that her organs could have been used to save other children? A number of professional "ethicists"—people employed by universities, hospitals, and law schools, who get paid to think about such things—were asked by the press to comment. Surprisingly few of them agreed with the parents and physicians. Instead, they appealed to time-honored philosophical principles to oppose taking the organs. "It just seems too horrifying to use people as means to other people's ends," said one such expert. Another explained: "It's unethical to kill person A to save person B." And a third added: "What the parents are really asking for is, Kill this dying baby so that its organs may be used for someone else. Well, that's really a horrendous proposition."

Is it horrendous? Opinions were divided. These ethicists thought so, while the parents and doctors did not. But we are interested in more than what people happen to think. We want to know what's true. Were the parents right or wrong to volunteer the baby's organs for transplant? To answer this question, we have to ask what reasons, or arguments, can be given for each side. What can be said to justify the parents' request or to justify thinking the request was wrong?

The Benefits Argument. The parents believed that Theresa's organs were doing her no good, because she was going to die soon anyway. The other children, however, could benefit from them. Thus, they seem to have reasoned: *If we can benefit someone, without harming anyone else, we ought to do so. Transplanting the organs would benefit the other children without harming Baby Theresa. Therefore, we ought to transplant the organs.*

Is this correct? Not every argument is sound. In addition to knowing what arguments can be given for a view, we also want to know whether those arguments are any good. Generally speaking, an argument is sound if its assumptions are true and the conclusion follows logically from them. In this case, we might wonder about the assertion that Theresa wouldn't be harmed. After all, she would die, and isn't being alive better than being dead? But on reflection, it seems clear that, in these tragic circumstances, the parents were right—being alive was doing her no good. Being alive is a benefit only if it enables you to carry on activities and have thoughts, feelings, and relations with other people—in other words, if it enables you to *have a life.* In the absence of such things, mere biological existence is worthless. Therefore, even though Theresa might remain alive for a few more days, it would do her no good.

The Benefits Argument, therefore, provides a powerful reason for transplanting the organs. What arguments are on the other side?

The Argument That We Should Not Use People as Means. The ethicists who opposed the transplants offered two arguments. The first was based on the idea that *it is wrong to use people as means to other people's ends.* Taking Theresa's organs would be using her to benefit the other children; therefore, it should not be done.

Is this argument sound? The idea that we should not "use" people is obviously appealing, but this is a vague notion that needs to be sharpened. What exactly does it mean? "Using people" typically involves violating their autonomy—their ability to decide for themselves how to live their own lives, according to their own desires and values. A person's autonomy may be violated through manipulation, trickery, or deceit. For example, I may pretend to be your friend, when I am only interested in going out with your sister; or I may lie to you so you'll give me money; or I may try to convince you that you will enjoy going to a movie, when I only want you to give me a ride. In each case, I am manipulating you in order to get something for myself. Autonomy is also violated when people are forced to do things against their will. This explains why "using people" is wrong; it is wrong because it thwarts people's autonomy.

Taking Baby Theresa's organs, however, could not thwart her autonomy, because she has no autonomy—she cannot make decisions, she has no desires, and she cannot value anything. Would it be "using her" in any other morally significant sense? We would, of course, be using her organs for someone else's benefit. But we do that every time we perform a transplant. We would also be using her organs without her permission. Would that make it wrong? If we were using them *against* her wishes, that would be a reason for objecting; it would violate her autonomy. But Baby Theresa has no wishes.

When people are unable to make decisions for themselves, and others must do it for them, there are two reasonable guidelines that might be adopted. First, we might ask, *What would be in their own best interests?* If we apply this standard to Baby Theresa, there would be no objection to taking her organs, for, as we have already noted, her interests will not be affected. She is not conscious, and she will die soon no matter what.

The second guideline appeals to the person's own preferences: We might ask, *If she could tell us what she wants, what would she say?* This sort of thought is useful when we are dealing with people who are known to have preferences but are unable to express them (for example, a comatose patient who has signed a living will). But, sadly, Baby Theresa has no preferences about anything, nor has she ever had any. So we can get no guidance from her, even in our imaginations. The upshot is that we are left to do what we think is best.

The Argument from the Wrongness of Killing. The ethicists also appealed to the principle that *it is wrong to kill one person to save another.* Taking Theresa's organs would be killing her to save others, they said; so, taking the organs would be wrong.

Is this argument sound? The prohibition against killing is certainly among the most important moral rules. Nevertheless, few people believe it is *always* wrong to kill—most people think there are exceptions, such as killing in self-defense. The question, then, is whether taking Baby Theresa's organs should be regarded as an exception to the rule. There are many reasons in favor of this: Baby Theresa is not conscious; she will never have a life; she is going to die soon anyway; and taking her organs would help the other babies. Anyone who accepts this will regard the argument as flawed. Usually, it is wrong to kill one person to save another, but not always.

There is another possibility. Perhaps the best way to understand the situation would be to regard Baby Theresa as already dead. If this sounds crazy, bear in mind that our conception of death has changed over the years. We now view death as occurring when the brain stops functioning. But this idea was initially resisted on the grounds that someone can be "brain dead" even though their heart and lungs still work. Eventually, however, brain death was accepted, and people came to regard it as "real" death. This was reasonable because when the brain dies, conscious life will never return.

Anencephalics do not meet the technical requirements for brain death as it is currently defined; but perhaps the definition should be revised to include them. After all, they also lack any hope for conscious life, because they have no cerebrum or cerebellum. If the definition of brain death were reformulated to include anencephalics, we would become accustomed to the idea that these unfortunate infants are born dead, and so taking their organs would not be killing them. The Argument from the Wrongness of Killing would then be moot.

On the whole, then, the arguments in favor of transplanting Baby Theresa's organs seem stronger than the arguments against it.

1.3. Second Example: Jodie and Mary

In August 2000, a young woman from Gozo, an island south of Italy, discovered that she was carrying conjoined twins. Knowing that health-care facilities on Gozo were inadequate to deal with the complications of such a birth, she and her husband went to St. Mary's Hospital in Manchester, England, to have the babies delivered. The infants, known as Mary and Jodie, were joined at the lower abdomen. Their spines were fused, and they had one heart and one pair of lungs between them. Jodie, the stronger one, was providing blood for her sister.

No one knows how many sets of conjoined twins are born each year, but the number has been estimated at 200. Most die shortly after birth, but some conjoined twins do well. They grow to adulthood and marry and have children themselves. But the outlook for Mary and Jodie was grim. The doctors said that without intervention the girls would die within six months. The only hope was an operation to separate them. This would save Jodie, but Mary would die immediately.

The parents, who were devout Catholics, refused permission for the operation on the grounds that it would hasten Mary's death. "We believe that nature should take its course," they said. "If it's God's will that both our children should not survive, then so be it." The hospital, hoping to save at least one of the infants, petitioned the courts for permission to separate them over the parents' objections. The courts granted permission, and the operation was performed. As expected, Jodie lived and Mary died.

In thinking about this case, we should distinguish the question of *who should make the decision* from the question of *what the decision should be.* You might think, for example, that the decision should be left to the parents, in which case you will object to the court's intrusion. But there remains the separate question of what would be the wisest choice for the parents (or anyone else) to make. We will focus on that question: Would it be right or wrong, in these circumstances, to separate the twins?

The Argument That We Should Save as Many as We Can. The rationale for separating the twins is that we have a choice between saving one infant or letting both die. Isn't it plainly better to save one? This argument is so appealing that many people will conclude, without further thought, that this settles the matter. At the height of the controversy, when the newspapers were full of stories about Jodie and Mary, the *Ladies' Home Journal* commissioned a poll to discover what Americans thought. The poll showed that 78% approved of the operation. People were obviously persuaded by the idea that we should save as many as we can. Jodie and Mary's parents, however, believed that there is an even stronger argument on the other side.

The Argument from the Sanctity of Human Life. The parents loved both of their children, and they thought it would be wrong to kill one of them even to save the other. Of course, they were not alone in thinking this. The idea that all human life is precious, regardless of age, race, social class, or handicap, is at the core of the Western moral tradition. It is especially emphasized in religious writings. In traditional ethics, the prohibition against killing innocent humans is absolute. It does not matter if the killing would serve a good purpose; it simply cannot be done. Mary is an innocent human being, and so she may not be killed.

Is this argument sound? The judges who heard the case did not think so, for a surprising reason. They denied that the rule against killing applies to this situation. Lord Justice Robert Walker said that in the course of the operation Mary would not be killed. She would merely be separated from her sister and then "She would die, not because she was intentionally killed, but because her own body cannot sustain her life." In other words, the operation wouldn't kill her; her body's weakness would. And so, the morality of killing is irrelevant.

The Lord Justice, however, has missed the point. It doesn't matter whether we say that Mary's death is caused by the operation or by her body's own weakness. Either way, she will be dead, and we will knowingly have hastened her death. *That's* the idea behind the traditional prohibition against killing the innocent.

There is, however, a more natural objection to the Argument from the Sanctity of Life. Perhaps it is *not* always wrong to kill innocent human beings. For example, such killings may be right when three conditions are met: (a) the innocent human has no future because she is going to die soon no matter what; (b) the innocent human has no wish to go on living, perhaps because she has no wishes at all; and (c) this killing will save others, who can go on to lead full lives. In these rare circumstances, the killing of the innocent might be justified.

1.4. Third Example: Tracy Latimer

Tracy Latimer, a 12-year-old victim of cerebral palsy, was killed by her father in 1993. Tracy lived with her family on a prairie farm in Saskatchewan, Canada. One Sunday morning while his wife and other children were at church, Robert Latimer put Tracy in the cab of his pickup truck and piped in exhaust fumes until she died. At the time of her death, Tracy weighed less than 40 pounds, and she was described as "functioning at the mental level of a three-month-old baby." Mrs. Latimer said that she was relieved to find Tracy dead when she arrived home and added that she "didn't have the courage" to do it herself.

Robert Latimer was tried for murder, but the judge and jury did not want to treat him harshly. The jury found him guilty of only second-degree murder and recommended that the judge ignore the mandatory 10-year sentence. The judge agreed and sentenced him to one year in prison, followed by a year of confinement to his farm. But the Supreme Court of Canada stepped in and ruled that the mandatory sentence must be imposed. Robert Latimer entered prison in 2001 and was paroled in 2008.

Legal questions aside, did Mr. Latimer do anything wrong? This case involves many of the issues that we saw in the other cases. One argument against Mr. Latimer is that Tracy's life was morally precious, and so he had no right to kill her. In his defense, it may be said that Tracy's condition was so catastrophic that she had no prospects of a "life" in any but a biological sense. Her existence had been reduced to pointless suffering, and so killing her was an act of mercy. Considering those arguments, it appears that Robert Latimer acted defensibly. There were, however, other points made by his critics.

The Argument from the Wrongness of Discriminating against the Handicapped. When Robert Latimer was given a lenient sentence by the trial court, many handicapped people took it as an insult. The president of the Saskatoon Voice of People with Disabilities, who has multiple sclerosis, said: "Nobody has the right to decide my life is worth less than yours. That's the bottom line." Tracy was killed because she was handicapped, he said, and that is unconscionable. Handicapped people should be given the same respect and the same rights as everyone else.

What are we to make of this? Discrimination against any group is a serious matter, because it involves treating some people worse than others, without any good justification. A common example involves discrimination in employment. Suppose a blind person is refused a job simply because the employer doesn't like the idea of hiring someone who can't see. This is no better than refusing to employ people because they are Hispanic or Jewish or female. Why is this person being treated differently? Is he less able to do the job? Is he less intelligent or less industrious? Does he deserve the job less? Is he less able to benefit from employment? If there is no good reason to exclude him, then it is arbitrary to do so.

Should we think of the death of Tracy Latimer as a case of discrimination against the handicapped? Robert Latimer argued that Tracy's cerebral palsy was not the issue: "People are saying this is a handicap issue, but they're wrong. This is a torture issue. It was about mutilation and torture for Tracy." Just before her death, Tracy had undergone major surgery on her back, hips, and legs, and more surgery was planned. "With the combination of a feeding tube, rods in her back, the leg cut and flopping around and bedsores," said her father, "how can people say she was a happy little girl?" At the trial, three of Tracy's physicians testified about the difficulty of controlling her pain. Thus, Mr. Latimer denied that Tracy was killed because of the cerebral palsy; she was killed because of her pain and suffering, and because there was no hope for her.

The Slippery Slope Argument. When the Canadian Supreme Court upheld Robert Latimer's sentence, the director of the Canadian Association of Independent Living Centres said that she was "pleasantly surprised." "It would have really been the slippery slope, and opening the doors to other people to decide who should live and who should die," she said.

Other disability advocates echoed this idea. We may feel sympathy for Robert Latimer, it was said; we may even think that Tracy Latimer is better off dead. However, it is dangerous to think like this. If we accept any sort of mercy killing, we will slide down a "slippery slope," and in the end all life will be held cheap. Where will we draw the line? If Tracy's life is not worth protecting, what about the lives of other disabled people? What about the elderly, the infirm, and other "useless" members of society? In this context, Hitler's program of "racial purification" is often mentioned, implying that, if we take the first step, we will end up like the Nazis.

Similar "slippery slope arguments" have been used in connection with all sorts of other issues. Abortion, in vitro fertilization (IVF), and most recently cloning have all been opposed because of what they might lead to. Sometimes, in hindsight, it is evident that the worries were unfounded. This has happened with IVF, a technique for creating embryos in the lab. When Louise Brown, the first "test tube baby," was born in 1978, there were dire predictions about what might be in store for her, her family, and society as a whole. But none of the predictions came true, and IVF has become routine. Since Louise Brown's birth, over 100,000 American couples have used IVF to have children.

When the future is unknown, however, it can be difficult to determine whether such an argument is sound. Reasonable people disagree about what would happen if mercy killing in cases like Tracy Latimer's were accepted. This kind of disagreement can be hard to resolve. Those inclined to defend Mr. Latimer may think the dire predictions are unrealistic, while those who want to condemn him may insist that the predictions are sensible.

It is worth noting, however, that this kind of argument is easy to abuse. If you are opposed to something but have no good arguments against it, you can always make up a prediction about what it might lead to; and no matter how implausible your prediction is, no one can prove you wrong. This method can be used to oppose almost anything. That is why such arguments should be approached with caution.

1.5. Reason and Impartiality

What can we learn from all this about the nature of morality? As a start, we may note two main points: first, moral judgments must be backed by good reasons; and second, morality requires the impartial consideration of each individual's interests.

Moral Reasoning. The cases of Baby Theresa, Jodie and Mary, and Tracy Latimer are liable to arouse strong feelings. Such feelings are often a sign of moral seriousness and may be admired. But they can also get in the way of discovering the truth: When we feel strongly about an issue, it is tempting to assume that we just *know* what the truth is, without even having to consider the arguments on the other side. Unfortunately, however, we cannot rely on our feelings, no matter how powerful they may be. Our feelings may be irrational; they may be nothing but the products of prejudice, selfishness, or cultural conditioning. At one time, for example, people's feelings told them that members of other races were inferior and that slavery was God's plan.

Moreover, people's feelings can be very different. In the case of Tracy Latimer, some people feel very strongly that her father should have been given a long prison term, while others feel equally strongly that he should never have been prosecuted. But both of these feelings cannot be correct.

Thus, if we want to discover the truth, we must let our feelings be guided as much as possible by reason. This is the essence of morality. The morally right thing to do is always the thing best supported by the arguments.

This is not a narrow point about a small range of moral views; it is a general requirement of logic that must be accepted by everyone regardless of their position on any particular issue. The fundamental point may be stated simply. Suppose someone says that you ought to do such-and-such. You may legitimately ask why you should do it, and if no good reason can be given, you may reject the advice as arbitrary or unfounded.

In this way, moral judgments are different from expressions of personal taste. If someone says, "I like coffee," she does not need to have a reason—she is merely stating a fact about herself, and nothing more. There is no such thing as "rationally defending" one's like or dislike of coffee. So long as she is accurately reporting her taste, what she says must be true. On the other hand, if someone says that something is morally wrong, he does need reasons, and if his reasons are legitimate, then other people must acknowledge their force. By the same logic, if he has no good reason for what he says, he is simply making noise, and we can ignore him.

Of course, not every reason that may be advanced is a good reason. There are bad arguments as well as good ones, and much of the skill of moral thinking consists in discerning the difference. But how do we tell the difference? How do we go about assessing arguments? The examples we have considered point to some answers.

The first thing is to get one's facts straight. Often this is not as easy as it sounds. Sometimes key facts are unknown. Other times, matters are so complex that even the experts disagree. Yet another problem is human prejudice. Often, we *want* to believe something because it supports our preconceptions. Those who disapprove of Robert Latimer's action, for example, will want to believe the predictions in the Slippery Slope Argument; those who approve of his actions will want to reject them. It is easy to think of other examples: People who do not want to give to charity often say that charities are inefficient, even when they have no good evidence for this; and people who dislike homosexuals may say that gay men are all pedophiles, even though very few are. But the facts exist independently of our wishes, and responsible moral thinking begins when we try to see things as they are.

Next, we can bring moral principles into play. In our three examples, a number of principles were involved: that we should not "use" people; that we should not kill one person to save another; that we should do what will benefit the people affected by our actions; that every life is sacred; and that it is wrong to discriminate against the handicapped. Most moral arguments consist of principles being applied to particular cases, and so we must ask whether the principles are justified and whether they are being applied correctly.

It would be nice if there were a simple recipe for constructing good arguments and avoiding bad ones. Unfortunately, there is no easy method. Arguments can go wrong in many ways, and we must always be alert to the possibility of new complications and new kinds of error. But that is not surprising. The rote application of routine methods is never a satisfactory substitute for critical thinking, in any area. Morality is no exception.

The Requirement of Impartiality. Almost every important theory of morality includes the idea of impartiality. This is the idea that each individual's interests are equally important; no one should get special treatment. At the same time, impartiality requires that we not treat the members of particular *groups* as inferior, and so practices such as sexism and racism are condemned.

The requirement of impartiality is closely connected with the point that moral judgments must be backed by good reasons. Consider the position of a racist who thinks that white people deserve all the good jobs. He would like all the doctors, lawyers, business executives, and so on, to be white. Now we can ask for reasons; we can ask why this is thought to be right. Is there something about white people that makes them better fitted for the highest-paying and most prestigious positions? Are they inherently brighter or more industrious? Do they care more about themselves and their families? Are they capable of benefiting more from the availability of such positions? In each case, the answer is no; and if there is no good reason for treating people differently, then discrimination is unacceptably arbitrary.

The requirement of impartiality, then, is at bottom nothing more than a rule against treating people arbitrarily. It forbids us from treating one person worse than another when there is no good reason to do so. But if this explains what is wrong with racism, it also explains why, in some cases, it is *not* racist to treat people differently. Suppose a movie director were making a film about Fred Shuttlesworth, the heroic African-American civil rights leader. This director would have a good reason not to cast Christian Bale in the starring role. Such "discrimination" would not be arbitrary and would not be open to criticism.

1.6. The Minimum Conception of Morality

We may now state the minimum conception: Morality is, at the very least, the effort to guide one's conduct by reason—that is, to do what there are the best reasons for doing—while giving equal weight to the interests of each individual affected by one's decision.

This gives us a picture of what it means to be a conscientious moral agent. The conscientious moral agent is someone who is concerned impartially with the interests of everyone affected by what he or she does; who carefully sifts facts and examines their implications; who accepts principles of conduct only after scrutinizing them to make sure they are justified; who is willing to "listen to reason" even when it means revising prior convictions; and who, finally, is willing to act on the results of this deliberation.

As one might expect, not every ethical theory accepts this "minimum." This picture of the moral agent has been disputed in various ways. However, theories that reject the minimum conception encounter serious difficulties. Most philosophers realize this, and so most theories of morality incorporate the minimum conception, in one form or another.

CHAPTER 2

The Challenge of Cultural Relativism

Morality differs in every society, and is a convenient term for socially approved habits.

RUTH BENEDICT, *PATTERNS OF CULTURE* (1934)

2.1. Different Cultures Have Different Moral Codes

Darius, a king of ancient Persia, was intrigued by the variety of cultures he met in his travels. He had found, for example, that the Callatians, who lived in India, ate the bodies of their dead fathers. The Greeks, of course, did not do that—the Greeks practiced cremation and regarded the funeral pyre as the natural and fitting way to dispose of the dead. Darius thought that a sophisticated outlook should appreciate the differences between cultures. One day, to teach this lesson, he summoned some Greeks who happened to be at his court and asked what it would take for them to eat the bodies of their dead fathers. They were shocked, as Darius knew they would be, and replied that no amount of money could persuade them to do such a thing. Then Darius called in some Callatians and, while the Greeks listened, asked them what it would take for them to burn their dead fathers' bodies. The Callatians were horrified and told Darius not to speak of such things.

This story, recounted by Herodotus in his *History*, illustrates a recurring theme in the literature of social science: Different cultures have different moral codes. What is thought right within one group may horrify the members of another group, and vice versa. Should we eat the bodies of the dead or burn them? If you were a Greek, one answer would seem

14

obviously correct; but if you were a Callatian, the other answer would seem certain.

There are many such examples. Consider the Eskimos of the early and mid 20th century. The Eskimos are the native people of Alaska, northern Canada, Greenland, and northeastern Siberia, in Asiatic Russia. Today, none of these groups call themselves "Eskimos," but the term has historically referred to that scattered Arctic population. Prior to the 20th century, the outside world knew little about them. Then explorers began to bring back strange tales.

The Eskimos lived in small settlements, separated by great distances, and their customs turned out to be very different from ours. The men often had more than one wife, and they would share their wives with guests, lending them out for the night as a sign of hospitality. Moreover, within a community, a dominant male might demand—and get—regular sexual access to other men's wives. The women, however, were free to break these arrangements simply by leaving their husbands and taking up with new partners—free, that is, so long as their former husbands chose not to make too much trouble. All in all, the Eskimo custom of marriage was a volatile practice that bore little resemblance to our custom.

But it was not only their marriages and sexual practices that were different. The Eskimos also seemed to have less regard for human life. Infanticide, for example, was common. Knud Rasmussen, an early explorer, reported that he met one woman who had borne 20 children but had killed 10 of them at birth. Female babies, he found, were especially likely to be killed, and this was permitted at the parents' discretion, with no social stigma attached. Moreover, when elderly family members became too feeble, they were left out in the snow to die. In Eskimo society, there seemed to be remarkably little respect for life.

Most of us would find these Eskimo customs completely immoral. Our own way of living seems so natural and right that we can hardly conceive of living so differently. When we hear of such things, we tend to categorize the other people as "backward" or "primitive." But to anthropologists, the Eskimos did not seem unusual. Since the time of Herodotus, enlightened observers have known that conceptions of right and wrong differ from culture to culture. If we assume that our ethical ideas will be shared by all cultures, we are merely being naïve.

2.2. Cultural Relativism

To many people, this observation—"Different cultures have different moral codes"—seems like the key to understanding morality. The idea of universal truth in ethics, they say, is a myth. The customs of different societies are all that exist. To say that a custom is "correct" or "incorrect" would imply that we can judge that custom by some independent standard of right and wrong. But no such standard exists, they say; every standard is culture-bound. The sociologist William Graham Sumner, writing in 1906, put it like this:

> The "right" way is the way which the ancestors used and which has been handed down. . . . The notion of right is in the folkways. It is not outside of them, of independent origin, and brought to test them. In the folkways, whatever is, is right. This is because they are traditional, and therefore contain in themselves the authority of the ancestral ghosts. When we come to the folkways we are at the end of our analysis.

This line of thought, more than any other, has persuaded people to be skeptical about ethics. Cultural Relativism, as it has been called, challenges our belief in the objectivity and universality of moral truth. It says, in effect, that there is no such thing as universal truth in ethics; there are only the various cultural codes, and nothing more.

The following claims have all been made by cultural relativists:

1. Different societies have different moral codes.
2. The moral code of a society determines what is right within that society; that is, if the moral code of a society says that a certain action is right, then that action *is* right, at least within that society.
3. There is no objective standard that can be used to judge one society's code as better than another's. There are no moral truths that hold for all people at all times.
4. The moral code of our own society has no special status; it is but one among many.
5. It is arrogant for us to judge other cultures. We should always be tolerant of them.

These five propositions may seem to go together, but they are independent of one another—some may be true while others are false. Indeed, two of the propositions appear to be inconsistent with each other. The second says that right and wrong are determined by the norms of a society; the fifth says that we should always be tolerant of other cultures. But what if the norms of a society favor intolerance? For example, when the Nazi army invaded Poland on September 1, 1939, thus beginning World War II, this was an intolerant action of the first order. But what if it was in line with Nazi ideals? A cultural relativist, it seems, cannot criticize the Nazis for being intolerant, if all they're doing is following their own moral code.

Given that cultural relativists take pride in their tolerance, it would be ironic if their theory actually supported the intolerance of warlike societies. However, it need not do that. Properly understood, Cultural Relativism holds that the norms of a culture reign supreme *within the bounds of the culture itself.* Thus, once the German soldiers entered Poland, they became bound by the norms of Polish society—norms that obviously excluded the mass slaughter of innocent Poles. "When in Rome," the old saying goes, "do as the Romans do." Cultural relativists agree.

2.3. The Cultural Differences Argument

Cultural Relativists often employ a certain *form of argument.* They begin with facts about cultures and end up drawing a conclusion about morality. Thus, they invite us to accept this reasoning:

> **(1)** The Greeks believed it was wrong to eat the dead, whereas the Callatians believed it was right to eat the dead.
>
> **(2)** Therefore, eating the dead is neither objectively right nor objectively wrong. It is merely a matter of opinion, which varies from culture to culture.

Or:

> **(1)** The Eskimos saw nothing wrong with infanticide, whereas Americans believe infanticide is immoral.

(2) Therefore, infanticide is neither objectively right nor objectively wrong. It is merely a matter of opinion, which varies from culture to culture.

Clearly, these arguments are variations of one fundamental idea. They are both examples of a more general argument, which says:

(1) Different cultures have different moral codes.

(2) Therefore, there is no objective "truth" in morality. Right and wrong are only matters of opinion, and opinions vary from culture to culture.

We may call this the Cultural Differences Argument. To many people, it is persuasive. But is it a good argument—is it *sound?*

It is not. For an argument to be sound, its premises must all be true, and the conclusion must follow logically from them. Here, the problem is that the conclusion does not follow from the premise—that is, even if the premise is true, the conclusion might still be false. The premise concerns what people *believe*—in some societies, people believe one thing; in other societies, people believe something else. The conclusion, however, concerns what *really is the case.* This sort of conclusion does not follow logically from that sort of premise. In philosophical terminology, this means that the argument is *invalid.*

Consider again the example of the Greeks and Callatians. The Greeks believed it was wrong to eat the dead; the Callatians believed it was right. Does it follow, *from the mere fact that they disagreed,* that there is no objective truth in the matter? No, it does not follow; it could be that the practice was objectively right (or wrong) and that one of them was simply mistaken.

To make the point clearer, consider a different matter. In some societies, people believe the earth is flat. In other societies, such as our own, people believe that the earth is spherical. Does it follow, from the mere fact that people disagree, that there is no "objective truth" in geography? Of course not; we would never draw such a conclusion, because we realize that the members of some societies might simply be wrong. There is no reason to think that if the world is round everyone must know it. Similarly, there is no reason to think that if there is moral truth everyone must know it. The Cultural Differences Argument tries to derive a substantive conclusion about a subject from the mere fact that people disagree. But this is impossible.

This point should not be misunderstood. We are not saying that the conclusion of the argument is false; Cultural Relativism could still be true. The point is that the conclusion does not follow from the premise. This means that the Cultural Differences Argument is invalid. Thus, the argument fails.

2.4. What Follows from Cultural Relativism

Even if the Cultural Differences Argument is unsound, Cultural Relativism might still be true. What would follow if it were true?

In the passage quoted earlier, William Graham Sumner states the essence of Cultural Relativism. He says that there is no measure of right and wrong other than the standards of one's society: "The notion of right is in the folkways. It is not outside of them, of independent origin, and brought to test them. In the folkways, whatever is, is right." Suppose we took this seriously. What would be some of the consequences?

1. *We could no longer say that the customs of other societies are morally inferior to our own.* This, of course, is one of the main points stressed by Cultural Relativism. We would have to stop condemning other societies merely because they are "different." So long as we concentrate on certain examples, such as the funerary practices of the Greeks and Callatians, this attitude may seem to be enlightened.

However, we would also be barred from criticizing other, less benign practices. For example, the Chinese government has a long history of repressing political dissent within its own borders. At any given time, thousands of political prisoners in China are doing hard labor, and in the Tiananmen Square episode of 1989, Chinese troops slaughtered hundreds, if not thousands, of peaceful protesters. Cultural Relativism would preclude us from saying that the Chinese government's policies of oppression are wrong. We could not even say that a society that respects free speech is *better* than Chinese society, for that would also imply a universal standard of comparison. The failure to condemn *these* practices does not seem enlightened; on the contrary, political oppression seems wrong wherever it occurs. Nevertheless, if we accept Cultural Relativism, we have to regard such social practices as immune from criticism.

2. *We could no longer criticize the code of our own society.* Cultural Relativism suggests a simple test for determining what is right and what is wrong: All we need to do is ask whether the action is in line with the code of the society in question. Suppose a resident of India wonders whether her country's caste system—a system of rigid social hierarchy—is morally correct. All she has to do is ask whether this system conforms to her society's moral code. If it does, there is nothing to worry about, at least from a moral point of view.

This implication of Cultural Relativism is disturbing because few of us think that our society's code is perfect—we can think of ways in which it might be improved. Moreover, we can think of ways in which we might learn from other cultures. Yet Cultural Relativism stops us from criticizing our own society's code, and it bars us from seeing ways in which other cultures might be better. After all, if right and wrong are relative to culture, this must be true for our culture, just as it is for other cultures.

3. *The idea of moral progress is called into doubt.* We think that at least some social changes are for the better. Throughout most of Western history, the place of women in society was narrowly defined. Women could not own property; they could not vote or hold political office; and they were under the almost absolute control of their husbands or fathers. Recently, much of this has changed, and most people think of it as progress.

But if Cultural Relativism is correct, can we legitimately view this as progress? Progress means replacing the old ways with new and improved ways. But by what standard do we judge the new ways as better? If the old ways conformed to the standards of *their* time, then Cultural Relativism would not judge them by *our* standards. Sexist 19th-century society was a different society from the one we have now. To say that we have made progress implies that present-day society is better—just the sort of transcultural judgment that Cultural Relativism forbids.

Our ideas about social *reform* will also have to be reconsidered. Reformers such as Martin Luther King, Jr., have sought to change their societies for the better. But according to Cultural Relativism, there is only one way to improve a society: to make it better match its own ideals. After all, the society's ideals are the standard by which reform is assessed. No one, however, may challenge the ideals themselves, for they are by definition correct. According to Cultural Relativism, then, the idea of social reform makes sense only in this limited way.

These three consequences of Cultural Relativism have led many thinkers to reject it. Slavery, they say, is wrong wherever it occurs, and one's own society can make fundamental moral progress. Because Cultural Relativism implies that these judgments make no sense, it cannot be right.

2.5. Why There Is Less Disagreement Than It Seems

Cultural Relativism starts by observing that cultures differ dramatically in their views of right and wrong. But how much do they really differ? It is true that there are differences, but it is easy to exaggerate them. Often, when we examine what seems to be a big difference, we find that the cultures differ less than we thought.

Consider a culture in which people believe it is wrong to eat cows. This may even be a poor culture, in which there is not enough food; still, the cows are not to be touched. Such a society would appear to have values very different from our own. But does it? We have not yet asked *why* these people will not eat cows. Suppose they believe that after death the souls of humans inhabit the bodies of animals, especially cows, so that a cow may be someone's grandmother. Shall we say that their values are different from ours? No; the difference lies elsewhere. The difference is in our belief systems, not in our values. We agree that we shouldn't eat Grandma; we disagree about whether the cow could be Grandma.

The point is that many factors work together to produce the customs of a society. Not only are the society's values important, but so are its religious beliefs, its factual beliefs, and its physical environment. We cannot conclude that, because customs differ, values differ. The difference in customs may be due to something else. Thus, there may be less disagreement about values than there appears to be.

Consider again the Eskimos, who killed perfectly healthy infants, especially girls. We do not approve of such things; in our society, a parent who kills a baby will be locked up. Thus, there appears to be a great difference in the values of our two cultures. But suppose we ask why the Eskimos did this. The explanation is not that they lacked respect for human life or did not love their children. An Eskimo family would always protect its babies if conditions permitted. But the Eskimos lived in a harsh environment, where food was in short supply. To quote an old Eskimo saying: "Life is hard, and the margin of safety small." A family may want to nourish its babies but be unable to do so.

As in many traditional societies, Eskimo mothers would nurse their infants over a much longer period than mothers in our culture—for four years, and perhaps even longer. So, even in the best of times, one mother could sustain very few children. Moreover, the Eskimos were nomadic; unable to farm in the harsh northern climate, they had to move about in search of food. Infants had to be carried, and a mother could carry only one baby in her parka as she traveled and went about her outdoor work. Finally, the Eskimos lacked birth control, so unwanted pregnancies were common.

Infant girls were more readily disposed of for two reasons. First, in Eskimo society, the males were the primary food providers—they were the hunters—and food was scarce. Infant boys were thus better protected. Second, the hunters suffered a high casualty rate, so the men who died prematurely far outnumbered the women who died young. If male and female infants had survived in equal numbers, then the female adult population would have greatly outnumbered the male adult population. Examining the available statistics, one writer concluded that "were it not for female infanticide . . . there would be approximately one-and-a-half times as many females in the average Eskimo local group as there are food-producing males."

So, among the Eskimos, infanticide did not signal a fundamentally different attitude toward children. Instead, it arose from the recognition that drastic measures were needed to ensure the family's survival. Even then, however, killing the baby was not the first option considered. Adoption was common; childless couples were especially happy to take a fertile couple's "surplus." Killing was the last resort. I emphasize this in order to show that the raw data of anthropology can be misleading; it can make the differences in values between cultures appear greater than they are. The Eskimos' values were not all that different from our own. It is only that life forced choices upon them that we do not have to make.

2.6. Some Values Are Shared by All Cultures

It should not be surprising that the Eskimos were protective of their children. How could they not be? Babies are helpless and cannot survive without extensive care. If a group did not protect its young, the young would not survive, and the older members of the group would not be replaced. After a while, the group would die out. This means that any culture that continues to exist must care for its young. Infants who are not cared for must be the exception rather than the rule.

Similar reasoning shows that other values must be more or less universal. Imagine what it would be like for a society to place no value on truth telling. When one person spoke to another, there would be no presumption that she was telling the truth, for she could just as easily be lying. Within that society, there would be no reason to pay attention to what anyone says. If I want to know what time it is, why should I bother asking anyone, if lying is commonplace? Communication would be extremely difficult, if not impossible, in such a society. And because societies cannot exist without communication among their members, society would become impossible. It follows that every society must value truthfulness. There may, of course, be situations in which lying is thought to be okay. No matter. The society will still value honesty.

Consider another example. Could a society exist in which there was no prohibition against murder? What would this be like? Suppose people were free to kill one another at will, and no one disapproved. In such a "society," no one could feel safe. Everyone would have to be constantly on guard, and to survive they would have to avoid other people as much as possible. This would result in individuals trying to become self-sufficient—after all, associating with others would be dangerous. Society on any large scale would collapse. Of course, people might band together in smaller groups where they could feel safe. But notice what this means: They would be forming smaller societies that did acknowledge a rule against murder. The prohibition against murder, then, is a necessary feature of society.

There is a general point here, namely, that *there are some moral rules that all societies must embrace, because those rules are necessary for society to exist.* The rules against lying and murder are two examples. And, in fact, we do find these rules in force in all cultures. Cultures may differ in what they regard as legitimate exceptions to the rules, but this disagreement exists against a broad background of agreement. Therefore, it is a mistake to overestimate the amount of difference between cultures. Not every moral rule can vary from society to society.

2.7. Judging a Cultural Practice to Be Undesirable

In 1996, a 17-year-old named Fauziya Kassindja arrived at Newark International Airport in New Jersey and asked for asylum. She had fled her native country of Togo, in West Africa, to escape what people there call "excision." Excision is a permanently disfiguring procedure. It is sometimes called "female circumcision," but it bears little resemblance to male circumcision. In the Western media, it is often referred to as "female genital mutilation."

According to the World Health Organization, excision is practiced in 28 African nations, and about 120 million females have been painfully excised. Sometimes, excision is part of an elaborate tribal ritual, performed in small villages, and girls look forward to it because it signals their acceptance into the adult world. Other times, the practice is carried out in cities on young women who desperately resist.

Fauziya Kassindja was the youngest of five daughters. Her father, who owned a successful trucking business, was opposed to excision, and he was able to defy the tradition because of his wealth. His first four daughters were married without being mutilated. But when Fauziya was 16, he suddenly died. She then came under the authority of her aunt, who arranged a marriage for her and prepared to have her excised. Fauziya was terrified, and her mother and oldest sister helped her escape.

In America, Fauziya was imprisoned for nearly 18 months while the authorities decided what to do with her. During this time, she was subjected to humiliating strip searches, denied medical treatment for her asthma, and generally treated like a criminal. Finally, she was granted asylum, but not before her case aroused a great controversy. The controversy was not about her treatment in America, but about how we should regard the cultural practices of other peoples. A series of articles in *The*

New York Times encouraged the idea that excision is barbaric and should be condemned. Other observers were reluctant to be so judgmental. Live and let live, they said; after all, our culture probably seems just as strange to other peoples.

Suppose we are inclined to say that excision is bad. Would we merely be imposing the standards of our own culture? If Cultural Relativism is correct, that is all we can do, for there is no culture-independent moral standard to appeal to. But is that true?

Is There a Culture-Independent Standard of Right and Wrong?
Excision is bad in many ways. It is painful and results in the permanent loss of sexual pleasure. Its short-term effects can include hemorrhage, tetanus, and septicemia. Sometimes the woman dies. Its long-term effects can include chronic infection, scars that hinder walking, and continuing pain.

Why, then, has it become a widespread social practice? It is not easy to say. The practice has no obvious social benefits. Unlike Eskimo infanticide, it is not necessary for group survival. Nor is it a matter of religion. Excision is practiced by groups from various religions, including Islam and Christianity.

Nevertheless, a number of reasons are given in its defense. Women who are incapable of sexual pleasure are less likely to be promiscuous; thus, there will be fewer unwanted pregnancies in unmarried women. Moreover, wives for whom sex is only a duty are less likely to cheat on their husbands; and because they are not thinking about sex, they will be more attentive to the needs of their husbands and children. Husbands, for their part, are said to enjoy sex more with wives who have been excised. Unexcised women, the men feel, are unclean and immature.

It would be easy, and perhaps a bit arrogant, to ridicule these arguments. But notice an important feature of them: They try to justify excision by showing that excision is beneficial—men, women, and their families are said to be better off when women are excised. Thus, we might approach the issue by asking whether this is true: Is excision, on the whole, helpful or harmful?

In fact, this is a standard that might reasonably be used in thinking about any social practice: *Does the practice promote or hinder the welfare of the people affected by it?* But this looks like just the sort of independent moral standard that Cultural Relativism says cannot exist. It is a single standard that may be brought to bear in judging the practices of any culture, at any time, including our own. Of course, people will not usually see this principle as being "brought in from the outside" to judge them, because all cultures value human happiness.

Why, Despite All This, Thoughtful People May Be Reluctant to Criticize Other Cultures. Many people who are horrified by excision are nevertheless reluctant to condemn it, for three reasons. First, there is an understandable nervousness about interfering in the social customs of other peoples. Europeans and their cultural descendants in America have a shameful history of destroying native cultures in the name of Christianity and enlightenment. Because of this, some people refuse to criticize other cultures, especially cultures that resemble those that were wronged in the past. There is a difference, however, between (a) judging a cultural practice to be deficient and (b) thinking that we should announce that fact, apply diplomatic pressure, and send in the troops. The first is just a matter of trying to see the world clearly, from a moral point of view. The second is something else entirely. Sometimes it may be right to "do something about it," but often it will not be.

Second, people may feel, rightly enough, that they should be tolerant of other cultures. Tolerance is, no doubt, a virtue—a tolerant person can live in peace with those who see things differently. But nothing about tolerance requires us to say that all beliefs, all religions, and all social practices are equally admirable. On the contrary, if we did not think that some things were better than others, there would be nothing for us to tolerate.

Finally, people may be reluctant to judge because they do not want to express contempt for the society being criticized. But again, this is misguided: To condemn a particular practice is not to say that the culture on the whole is contemptible or is inferior to any other culture. The culture could have many admirable features. In fact, we should expect this to be true of most human societies—they are mixtures of good and bad practices. Excision happens to be one of the bad ones.

2.8. Back to the Five Claims

Let us now return to the five tenets of Cultural Relativism that were listed earlier. How have they fared in our discussion?

1. Different societies have different moral codes.

This is certainly true, although there are some values that all cultures share, such as the value of truth telling, the importance of caring for the young, and the prohibition against murder. Also, when customs differ, the underlying reason will often have more to do with the factual beliefs of the cultures than with their values.

2. The moral code of a society determines what is right within that society; that is, if the moral code of a society says that a certain action is right, then that action *is* right, at least within that society.

Here we must bear in mind the difference between what a society *believes* about morals and what is *really true*. The moral code of a society is closely tied to what people in that society believe to be right. However, that code, and those people, can be in error. Earlier, we considered the example of excision—a barbaric practice endorsed by many societies. Consider three more examples, all of which involve the mistreatment of women:

- In 2002, an unwed mother in Nigeria was sentenced to be stoned to death for having had sex out of wedlock. It is unclear whether Nigerian values, on the whole, approved of this verdict, since it was later overturned by a higher court. However, it was overturned partly to appease the international community. When the Nigerians themselves heard the verdict being read out in the courtroom, the crowd shouted out their approval.
- In 2005, a woman from Australia was convicted of trying to smuggle nine pounds of marijuana into Indonesia. For that crime, she was sentenced to 20 years in prison—an excessive punishment. Under Indonesian law, she might even have received a death sentence.
- In 2007, a woman was gang-raped in Saudi Arabia. When she complained to the police, the police discovered in the course of their investigation that she had recently

been alone with a man she was not related to. For this crime, she was sentenced to ninety lashes. When she appealed the conviction, this angered the judges, and they increased her sentence to 200 lashes plus a six-month prison term. Eventually, the Saudi king pardoned her, though he said that he supported the sentence she had received.

Cultural Relativism holds, in effect, that societies are morally infallible—in other words, that the morals of a culture can never be wrong. But when we see that societies can and do endorse grave injustices, we see that societies, like their members, can be in need of moral improvement.

3. There is no objective standard that can be used to judge one society's code as better than another's. There are no moral truths that hold for all people at all times.

It is difficult to think of ethical principles that hold for all people at all times. However, if we are to criticize the practice of slavery, or stoning, or genital mutilation, and if such practices are really and truly wrong, then we must appeal to principles that are not tethered to one society's peculiar outlook. Earlier I suggested one such principle: that it always matters whether a practice promotes or hinders the welfare of the people affected by it.

4. The moral code of our own society has no special status; it is but one among many.

It is true that the moral code of our society has no special status. After all, our society has no heavenly halo around its borders; our values do not have any special standing just because we happen to believe them. However, to say that the moral code of one's own society "is merely one among many" seems to deny the possibility that one moral code might be better or worse than some others. Whether the moral code of one's own society "is merely one among many" is, in fact, an open question. That code might be one of the best; it might be one of the worst.

5. It is arrogant for us to judge other cultures. We should always be tolerant of them.

There is much truth in this, but the point is overstated. We *are* often arrogant when we criticize other cultures, and tolerance *is* generally a good thing. However, we shouldn't tolerate everything. Human societies have done terrible things, and it is a mark of progress when we can say that those things are in the past.

2.9. What We Can Learn from Cultural Relativism

So far, in discussing Cultural Relativism, I have dwelt mostly on its shortcomings. I have said that it rests on an unsound argument, that it has implausible consequences, and that it suggests greater moral disagreement than exists. This all adds up to a rather thorough repudiation of the theory. Nevertheless, you may have the feeling that all this is a little unfair. The theory must have something going for it—why else has it been so influential? In fact, I think there is something right about Cultural Relativism, and there are two lessons we should learn from it.

First, Cultural Relativism warns us, quite rightly, about the danger of assuming that all our preferences are based on some absolute rational standard. They are not. Many (but not all) of our practices are merely peculiar to our society, and it is easy to lose sight of that fact. In reminding us of it, the theory does us a service.

Funerary practices are one example. The Callatians, according to Herodotus, were "men who eat their fathers"—a shocking idea, to us at least. But eating the flesh of the dead could be understood as a sign of respect. It could be taken as a symbolic act that says, "We wish this person's spirit to dwell within us." Perhaps this is how the Callatians saw it. On this way of thinking, burying the dead could be seen as an act of rejection, and burning the corpse as positively scornful. Of course, we may feel a visceral repugnance at the idea of eating human flesh. But so what? This repugnance may be, as the relativists say, only a reflection of our own society.

There are many other matters that we tend to think of in terms of right and wrong that are really nothing more than social conventions. Consider monogamous marriage. Why must we lock ourselves into just one romantic relationship? Some people practice "polyamory," which is having more than one loving partner, with the consent of everyone involved. Polyamory includes group marriages (such as "quads," involving four people), open relationships, networks of interconnecting relationships, and so on. Some of these arrangements might work better than others, but this is not really a matter of morality. If four people want to live together and function as a single family, with love flowing from each to each, there is nothing morally wrong with that. But most people in our society would be horrified by it.

Or consider modesty of dress. During the 2004 Super Bowl halftime show, Justin Timberlake ripped off part of Janet Jackson's costume, thus exposing one of her breasts to the audience. CBS quickly cut to an aerial view of the stadium, but it was too late. Half a million viewers complained, and the federal government fined CBS $550,000. In America, a publicly exposed breast is considered scandalous. In other cultures, however, such displays are common. Objectively speaking, the display of a woman's breast is neither right nor wrong. Cultural Relativism begins with the valuable insight that many of our practices are like this—they are only cultural products. Then it goes wrong by inferring that, because some practices are like this, all of them must be.

The second lesson has to do with keeping an open mind. In the course of growing up, each of us has acquired some strong feelings: We have learned to think of some types of conduct as acceptable, and we have learned to reject others. Occasionally, we may find those feelings challenged. For example, we may have been taught that homosexuality is immoral, and we may feel uncomfortable around gay people and see them as alien and perverted. But then someone suggests that this may be prejudice; that there is nothing wrong with homosexuality; that gay people are just people, like anyone else, who happen to be attracted to members of the same sex. Because we feel so strongly about this, we may find it hard to take this line of reasoning seriously.

Cultural Relativism provides an antidote for this kind of dogmatism. When he tells the story of the Greeks and Callatians, Herodotus adds:

> For if anyone, no matter who, were given the opportunity
> of choosing from amongst all the nations of the world

the set of beliefs which he thought best, he would inevitably, after careful consideration of their relative merits, choose that of his own country. Everyone without exception believes his own native customs, and the religion he was brought up in, to be the best.

Realizing this can help broaden our minds. We can see that our feelings are not necessarily perceptions of the truth—they may be nothing more than the result of cultural conditioning. Thus, when we hear it suggested that some element of our social code is *not* really the best, and we find ourselves resisting the suggestion, we might stop and remember this. Then we will be more open to discovering the truth, whatever it might be.

We can understand the appeal of Cultural Relativism, then, despite its shortcomings. It is an attractive theory because it is based on a genuine insight: that many of the practices and attitudes we find natural are really only cultural products. Moreover, keeping this thought firmly in view is important if we want to avoid arrogance and keep an open mind. These are important points, not to be taken lightly. But we can accept them without accepting the whole theory.

CHAPTER 3

Subjectivism in Ethics

Take any [vicious] action. . . . Wilful murder, for instance. Examine it in all lights, and see if you can find that matter of fact, or real existence, which you call vice. . . . You can never find it, till you turn your reflexion into your own breast, and find a sentiment of [disapproval], which arises in you, toward this action. Here is a matter of fact; but 'tis the object of feeling, not reason.

DAVID HUME, *A TREATISE OF HUMAN NATURE* (1740)

3.1. The Basic Idea of Ethical Subjectivism

In 2001 there was a mayoral election in New York, and when it came time for the city's Gay Pride Day parade, every single Democratic and Republican candidate showed up to march. Matt Foreman, the executive director of a gay rights organization, described all the candidates as "good on our issues." He said, "In other parts of the country, the positions taken here would be extremely unpopular, if not deadly, at the polls." The national Republican Party apparently agrees; at the urging of religious conservatives, it has made opposition to gay rights a part of its agenda.

What do people around the country actually think? Since 1982, the Gallup Poll has been asking Americans, "Do you feel that homosexuality should be considered an acceptable alternative lifestyle or not?" In 1982, only 34% said it should be; by 2008, the number had risen to 57%. The Gallup Poll has also been asking people whether they personally believe homosexual relations to be morally acceptable or morally wrong. In 2001, 53%–40% called homosexual relations "morally wrong"; in 2008, the public was divided 48%–48%.

People on both sides have strong feelings. The late Reverend Jerry Falwell spoke for many when he said in a television interview, "Homosexuality is immoral. The so-called 'gay rights' are not rights at all, because immorality is not right." Falwell was a Baptist. The Catholic view is more nuanced, but it agrees that gay sex is impermissible. Gays and lesbians, according to the *Catechism of the Catholic Church,* "do not choose their homosexual condition" and "must be accepted with respect, compassion, and sensitivity. Every sign of unjust discrimination in their regard should be avoided." Nonetheless, "homosexual acts are intrinsically disordered" and "under no circumstances can they be approved." Therefore, to lead virtuous lives, homosexuals must not act on their desires.

What attitude should we take? We might say that homosexuality is immoral, or we might say it is acceptable. But there is a third alternative. We might say:

> People have different opinions, but where morality is concerned, there are no "facts," and no one is "right." People just feel differently, and that's all there is to it.

This is the basic thought behind Ethical Subjectivism. Ethical Subjectivism is the idea that our moral opinions are based on our feelings and nothing more. On this view, there is no such thing as "objective" right or wrong. It is a fact that some people are homosexual and some are heterosexual; but it is not a fact that one is good and the other is bad. So, when someone such as Falwell says that homosexuality is wrong, he is not stating a fact about homosexuality. Instead, he is merely saying something about his feelings.

Of course, Ethical Subjectivism is not merely an idea about the evaluation of homosexuality. It applies to all moral matters. To take a different example, it is a fact that the Nazis exterminated millions of innocent people; but according to Ethical Subjectivism, it is not a fact that what they did was evil. When we say that their actions were evil, we are only saying that we have negative feelings toward them. The same applies to any moral judgment whatever.

3.2. The Evolution of the Theory

A philosophical theory may go through several stages. At first, it is put forward in simple, crude terms, which many people find attractive. That simple formulation, however, is analyzed and found to have defects. At this point, some people are so impressed with the objections that they abandon the theory. Others, however, retain confidence in the basic idea, and so they refine it. For a while, it looks like the theory has been saved. But then further arguments cast doubt on the new version. Those new objections, like the old, cause some people to abandon the idea, while others keep the faith and propose another "improved" version. The whole process of revision and criticism then begins again.

The theory of Ethical Subjectivism has developed in just this way. It began as a simple idea—in the words of David Hume, that morality is a matter of sentiment rather than fact. But as objections were raised to the theory, and as its defenders tried to answer the objections, the theory became more sophisticated.

3.3. The First Stage: Simple Subjectivism

The simplest version of the theory is this: When a person says that something is morally good or bad, this means that he or she approves of that thing, or disapproves of it, and nothing more. In other words:

"X is morally acceptable"
"X is right"
"X is good"   all mean: "I (the speaker)
"X ought to be done"   approve of X"

And similarly:

"X is morally unacceptable"
"X is wrong"
"X is bad"   all mean: "I (the speaker)
"X ought not to be done"   disapprove of X"

We may call this version of the theory Simple Subjectivism. It expresses the basic idea of Ethical Subjectivism in a plain, uncomplicated form, and many people have found it attractive. However, it is open to some serious objections.

Simple Subjectivism Cannot Account for Disagreement. Gay rights advocate Matt Foreman does not believe that homosexuality is immoral. Baptist Minister Jerry Falwell, however, thinks it is immoral. So, it would seem that Foreman and Falwell disagree. But consider what Simple Subjectivism implies about this situation.

According to Simple Subjectivism, when Foreman says that homosexuality is not immoral, he is merely making a statement about his attitudes—he is saying, "I, Matt Foreman, do not disapprove of homosexuality." Would Falwell disagree with that? No, Falwell would agree that Foreman does not disapprove of homosexuality. At the same time, when Falwell says that homosexuality is immoral, he is only saying, "I, Jerry Falwell, disapprove of homosexuality." And how could anyone disagree with that? Thus, according to Simple Subjectivism, there is no disagreement between them; each should acknowledge the truth of what the other is saying. Surely, though, this is incorrect, because Falwell and Foreman *do* disagree about homosexuality.

There is a kind of eternal frustration implied by Simple Subjectivism: Falwell and Foreman are deeply opposed to one another, yet they cannot even state their positions in a way that gets at the issue. Foreman may try to deny what Falwell says, but according to Simple Subjectivism, he succeeds only in changing the subject.

The argument may be summarized like this: When one person says, "X is morally acceptable," and someone else says, "X is morally unacceptable," they are disagreeing. However, if Simple Subjectivism were correct, there would be no disagreement between them. Therefore, Simple Subjectivism cannot be correct.

Simple Subjectivism Implies That We're Always Right. We are sometimes wrong in our moral evaluations. But if Simple Subjectivism were correct, this would be impossible.

Again, consider Falwell, who said that homosexuality is immoral. According to Simple Subjectivism, he was merely saying that he, Falwell, disapproves of homosexuality. Of course, he might have been speaking insincerely—it is possible that he didn't really mind homosexuality but was merely playing to his conservative audience. However, if Falwell was speaking sincerely, then what he said was true. So long as someone is honestly representing his own feelings, his moral judgments will always be correct. But this contradicts the plain fact that we sometimes make mistakes. Therefore, Simple Subjectivism cannot be correct.

These arguments, and others like them, show that Simple Subjectivism is a flawed theory. It cannot be maintained, at least not in such a crude form. In the face of such arguments, some thinkers have chosen to reject the whole idea of Ethical Subjectivism. Others, however, have worked to improve the theory.

3.4. The Second Stage: Emotivism

The improved version came to be known as Emotivism. Emotivism was popular during the mid-20th century, largely due to the work of the American philosopher Charles L. Stevenson (1908–1979).

Language, Stevenson said, is used in many ways. One way is to make statements—that is, to state facts. Thus we may say:

> "Gas prices are rising."
> "Lance Armstrong beat cancer and then won the Tour de France bike race seven times."
> "Shakespeare wrote *Hamlet*."

In each case, we are saying something that is either true or false, and the purpose of our utterance is, typically, to convey information to the listener.

However, language is also used for other purposes. Suppose I say, "Close the door!" This utterance is neither true nor false. It is not a statement, intended to convey information; it is a command, which is something different. Its purpose is to get the listener to do something.

Or consider utterances such as these, which are neither statements nor commands:

> "Aaargh!"
> "Way to go, Lance!"
> "Damn Hamlet!"

We understand these sentences easily enough. But none of them can be true or false. (It makes no sense to say, "It is true that way to go, Lance" or "It is false that aaargh.") These sentences are not used to state facts or to influence behavior. Their purpose is to express the speaker's attitudes—about gas prices, about Lance Armstrong, or about Hamlet.

Now let us turn our attention to moral language. According to Simple Subjectivism, which we discussed earlier, moral language is about stating facts—ethical statements report the speaker's attitudes. According to Simple Subjectivism, when Falwell says, "Homosexuality is immoral," his utterance means "I (Falwell) disapprove of homosexuality"—a statement of fact about Falwell's attitude.

According to Emotivism, however, moral language is not fact-stating language; it is not used to convey information or to make reports. It is used, first, as a means of influencing people's behavior. If someone says, "You shouldn't do that," he is trying to *persuade you not to do it*. Thus, the utterance is more like a command than a statement of fact; "You shouldn't do that" is like saying "Don't do that!" Also, moral language is used to express one's attitudes. Saying "Lance Armstrong is a good man" is like saying "Way to go, Lance!" It is *not* like saying "Lance Armstrong is 5'10"." It is not a factual remark. And so, when Falwell says, "Homosexuality is immoral," emotivists interpret his utterance as equivalent to something like "Homosexuality—gross!" or "Don't be gay!"

This difference between Simple Subjectivism and Emotivism may seem trivial. But it is important. To see why, consider again the arguments against Simple Subjectivism. While those arguments were severely embarrassing to Simple Subjectivism, they are less effective against Emotivism.

1. The first argument had to do with moral disagreement. If Simple Subjectivism is correct, then when one person says, "X is morally acceptable," and someone else says, "X is morally unacceptable," they are not really disagreeing. They are, in fact, talking about different things—each is making a statement about his or her own attitude, and the other person can readily agree. But, the argument goes, people who say such things really are disagreeing, and so Simple Subjectivism cannot be correct.

In response, Emotivism emphasizes that disagreement comes in different forms. Compare these two kinds of disagreement:

- I believe that Lee Harvey Oswald acted alone in the assassination of President John F. Kennedy, and you believe there was a conspiracy. This is a disagreement about the facts—I believe something to be true that you believe to be false.

- I am rooting for the Atlanta Braves to win, and you want them to lose. Our beliefs are not in conflict, but our desires are—I want something to happen that you want not to happen.

In the first kind of disagreement, we believe different things, both of which cannot be true. In the second, we want different things, both of which cannot happen. Stevenson calls the second kind of disagreement *disagreement in attitude,* and he contrasts it with disagreement *about* attitudes. You and I may agree in all our judgments about our attitudes: We agree that I am rooting for the Braves just because I am from the South; we agree that the Braves' players are overpaid; we agree that Atlanta is not a great baseball town, and so on. But we still disagree *in* our attitudes. Moral disagreements, says Stevenson, are like that: They are disagreements *in* attitude. Simple Subjectivism could not explain moral disagreement because, once it interpreted moral judgments as statements *about* attitudes, the disagreement vanished. Emotivism does not have that problem.

2. The second argument was that if Simple Subjectivism is correct, then we are always right in our moral judgments. But, of course, we are not always right. Therefore, Simple Subjectivism cannot be correct.

This argument is effective only because Simple Subjectivism interprets moral judgments as statements that can be true or false. "Always right" means that one's judgments are always true; and Simple Subjectivism assigns moral judgments a meaning that *will* always be true, so long as the speaker is sincere. That is why, on that theory, people turn out to be right all the time. Emotivism, on the other hand, does not interpret moral judgments as statements that are true or false, and so the same argument will not work against it. Because commands and expressions of attitude cannot be true or false, people cannot "be right" with respect to them, much less be right all the time.

Emotivism, then, also avoids this objection to Simple Subjectivism. However, it is susceptible to a related complaint. Although we're not always right in our evaluations, we're right some of the time. Sometimes our moral judgments are true and sometimes they are false. Emotivists, however, cannot say this, since they deny that moral discourse is about stating facts.

Consider this example. On January 26, 2004, an 8-year-old girl named Katie Shelton was walking down a street in Seymour, Indiana. Suddenly, she was confronted by two rottweilers, each weighing over 80 pounds. The dogs knocked Katie down and bit her repeatedly. The little girl's life, however, was saved by the heroic actions of 14-year-old Mark Friedrich, who lived nearby. When Mark saw what was going on, he rushed out of his family's house with two sticks and attacked the dogs. Predictably, Mark got bitten, but he was able to keep the dogs off Katie until a police officer arrived with a gun. Both children recovered from their wounds (the dogs were not so lucky).

Now suppose that, upon hearing this story, someone said that Mark Friedrich acted badly: "If he was a good kid, he would have minded his own business and kept watching television." As long as this strange person was speaking sincerely, the Simple Subjectivist would have to say that his moral judgment was *true.* The emotivist's position is different, but like the Simple Subjectivist, he is barred from saying that this person's judgment is false. He must say that the person is merely expressing his feelings.

Although Emotivism is an improvement on Simple Subjectivism, both theories imply that our moral judgments are, in a sense, beyond reproach. For Simple Subjectivism, our judgments cannot be criticized because they will always be true. For Emotivism, our moral judgments cannot be criticized because they are not judgments at all; they are mere expressions of attitude, which cannot be false. That is one problem for Emotivism. Another problem is that Emotivism cannot explain the role reason plays in ethics.

3.5. The Role of Reason in Ethics

If someone says, "I like peaches," she does not need to have a reason; she may be making a statement about her personal taste and nothing more. But moral judgments are different. If someone tells you that a particular act would be wrong, you may ask why, and if there is no satisfactory answer, then you may reject that advice as unfounded. A moral judgment—or for that matter, any kind of value judgment—must be supported by good reasons. Any adequate theory of ethics should be able to explain how reasons can support moral judgments.

What do emotivists say about reasons? Remember that for the emotivist, moral judgments have two functions: to express one's attitudes, and to try to influence other people's attitudes and conduct. Can the expressive function of moral language find a place for reasons? Insofar as moral judgments are mere expressions of attitude, they are like personal preferences. When I say, "Liberty is morally better than slavery," the emotivist hears this as similar to "Peaches are better than apples." The emotivist will recognize some differences between those two utterances. However, they are basically alike. Reason can play no important role here.

Thus, emotivists have usually looked to the command function of moral language to find a role for reasons. Suppose I had said to you in 2008, "You shouldn't vote for Obama." If this utterance is like a command—if it is like saying, "Don't vote for Obama"—then what role can reasons play in such a judgment? If I am trying to influence your conduct, then perhaps the emotivist should say that a reason is any consideration that will influence your conduct. But consider what this means. Suppose I know that you are prejudiced against Muslims. And I say, "Obama, you know, is a Muslim." That does the trick; you now decide not to vote for Obama. For the emotivist, the claim that Obama is a Muslim would be, given the right audience, a moral reason not to vote for him. In fact, Stevenson takes exactly this view. In his classic work *Ethics and Language* (1944), he says, "*Any* statement about *any* fact which *any* speaker considers likely to alter attitudes may be adduced as a reason for or against an ethical judgment."

Obviously, something has gone wrong. Not just any claim can count as a reason in support of just any judgment. For one thing, it must be relevant to the judgment, and psychological influence does not always bring relevance with it. Being Muslim is irrelevant to one's ability to be a good president, regardless of the psychological connections in anyone's mind. Also, to be a legitimate reason, a claim must be true, and yet false claims can be persuasive. President Obama is not in fact a Muslim.

There are two lessons to be learned from this. The small lesson is that a particular moral theory, Emotivism, is flawed, which casts doubt on the whole idea of Ethical Subjectivism.

The larger lesson has to do with the importance of reason in ethics.

Hume emphasized that if we examine wicked actions—"wilful murder, for instance"—we will find no "matter of fact" corresponding to the wickedness. The universe, apart from our attitudes, contains no such facts. What can we conclude from this? Admittedly, values are not tangible things like planets and trees and spoons. But this does not mean that ethics has no objective basis. A fundamental mistake, which many people fall into, is to assume just two possibilities:

1. There are moral facts, in the same way that there are planets and trees and spoons.
2. Our values are nothing more than the expression of our subjective feelings.

This is a mistake because it overlooks a third possibility. People have not only feelings but reason, and that makes a big difference. It may be that

3. Moral truths are truths of reason; that is, a moral judgment is true if it is backed by better reasons than the alternatives.

On this view, moral truths are objective in the sense that they are true independently of what we might want or think. We cannot make something good or bad just by wishing it so, because we cannot will that the weight of reason be on its side or against it. And this also explains our fallibility: We can be wrong about what is good or bad because we can be wrong about what reason recommends. Reason says what it says, regardless of our opinions or desires.

3.6. Are There Proofs in Ethics?

If Ethical Subjectivism is not true, why are so many people attracted to it? One reason is that science provides our paradigm of objectivity, and when we compare ethics to science, ethics seems lacking. For example, there are proofs in science, but there are no proofs in ethics. We can prove that the world is round, that dinosaurs lived before humans, and that there is no largest prime number. But we can't prove that abortion is acceptable or unacceptable.

The general idea that moral judgments can't be proved sounds appealing. Anyone who has ever argued about a matter like abortion knows how frustrating it can be to try to "prove" one's opinion. However, if we inspect this idea more closely, it turns out to be suspect.

Suppose we consider something much simpler than abortion. A student says that a test given by a teacher was unfair. This is clearly a moral judgment—fairness is a basic moral value. Can this judgment be proved? The student might point out that the test covered a lot of material that was trivial while it ignored material the teacher had stressed as important. The test also included questions about material that was not covered in either the readings or the class discussions. Moreover, the test was so long that even the best students could not complete it in the time allowed.

Suppose all this is true. And further suppose that the teacher, when asked to explain, can offer no defense. In fact, the teacher, who is rather inexperienced, seems confused about the whole thing. Now, hasn't the student proved that the test was unfair? What more in the way of proof could we want? It is easy to think of other examples that make the same point:

- *Jones is a bad man:* Jones is a habitual liar; he toys with people; he cheats when he thinks he can get away with it; he once killed someone in a dispute over 37 cents; and so on.
- *Dr. Smith is irresponsible:* He bases his diagnoses on superficial considerations; he refuses to listen to other doctors' advice; he drinks beer before performing delicate surgery; and so on.
- *A certain used-car dealer is unethical:* She conceals defects in her cars; she takes advantage of poor people by pressuring them into paying exorbitant prices; she runs misleading advertisements on the Web; and so on.

The process of giving reasons might even be taken one step further. If we criticize Jones for being a habitual liar, we can go on to explain why lying is bad. Lying is bad, first, because it harms people. If I give you false information, and you rely on it, things may go wrong for you in all sorts of ways. Second, lying is bad because it is a violation of trust. Trusting another person means leaving oneself vulnerable and unprotected. When I trust you, I simply believe what you say, without taking precautions; and when you lie, you take advantage of my trust. And finally, the rule requiring truthfulness is necessary for society to exist—if we could not assume that other people would speak truthfully, communication would be impossible, and if communication were impossible, society would fall apart.

So we can support our judgments with good reasons, and we can provide explanations of why those reasons matter. If we can do all this, and, for an encore, show that no comparable case can be made on the other side, what more in the way of "proof" could anyone want? It is absurd to say, in the face of all this, that ethical judgments can be nothing more than "mere opinions."

Nevertheless, the impression that moral judgments are "unprovable" is remarkably persistent. Why do people believe this? Three points might be raised.

First, when proof is demanded, people often want scientific proof. They are thinking about observation and experimentation; and because there are no such methods in ethics, they conclude that there is no proof. But in ethics, rational thinking consists in giving reasons, analyzing arguments, setting out and justifying principles, and so on. The fact that ethical reasoning differs from scientific reasoning does not make it deficient.

Second, when we think about proving our ethical opinions, we tend to think of the most difficult issues. The question of abortion, for example, is enormously complicated. If we consider only issues like abortion, it is easy to believe that "proof" in ethics is impossible. But the same could be said of the sciences. There are complicated matters that physicists cannot agree on; and if we focused entirely on them, we might conclude that there are no proofs in physics. But, of course, there are many simpler issues on which all physicists agree. Similarly, in ethics, there are many simple issues about which all reasonable people agree.

Finally, it is easy to run together two matters that are really very different:

1. Proving an opinion to be correct
2. Persuading someone to accept your proof

An argument may be perfect yet fall on deaf ears. When this happens, it should not be surprising. Ethics tells people to do things they don't want to do; sometimes people don't want to listen. We cannot conclude from this that proof in ethics is unattainable.

3.7. The Question of Homosexuality

We can conclude by returning to the dispute about homosexuality. If we consider the relevant reasons, what do we find? The most pertinent fact is that homosexuals are pursuing the only way of life that affords them a chance of happiness. Sex is a particularly strong urge, and few people can be happy without satisfying their sexual needs. We should not, however, focus simply on sex. More than one gay writer has said that homosexuality is not about who you have sex with; it's about who you fall in love with. Achieving the good life, for gays and lesbians as well as for everyone else, may mean building a life with someone you love. Moreover, individuals do not choose their sexual orientations; both homosexuals and heterosexuals find themselves to be what they are without having decided to be that way. Thus, to say that people should not express their homosexuality is, more often than not, to condemn them to unhappy lives.

If it could be shown that gays and lesbians pose some sort of threat to the rest of society, that would be a powerful argument for the other side. And, in fact, people who share Jerry Falwell's view have often claimed as much. But when examined objectively, those claims always turn out to have no factual basis. There is no difference between homosexuals and heterosexuals in their moral characters or in their contributions to society. The idea that homosexuals are dangerous proves to be a myth similar to the myth that black people are lazy or that Muslims are terrorists.

The case against homosexuality thus reduces to the claim that it is "unnatural" or to the claim often made by religious conservatives that it threatens "family values." It is hard to know what to make of the first claim because the notion of "unnaturalness" is unclear. What exactly does it mean? There are at least three possible meanings.

First, "unnatural" might be taken as a statistical notion. In this sense, a human quality is unnatural if it is not shared by most people. Being gay would be unnatural in this sense, but so would being left-handed, being tall, and even being immensely nice. Clearly, this is no reason to criticize homosexuality. Rare qualities are often good.

Second, the meaning of "unnatural" might be connected with the idea of a thing's *purpose*. The parts of our bodies seem to serve particular purposes. The purpose of the eyes is to see, and the purpose of the heart is to pump blood. Similarly, the purpose of our genitals is to procreate: Sex is for making babies. It may be argued, then, that gay sex is unnatural because it is sexual activity that is divorced from its natural purpose.

This seems to express what many people have in mind when they object to homosexuality as unnatural. However, if gay sex were condemned for this reason, a number of other, widely accepted practices would also have to be condemned: masturbation, oral sex, sex using condoms, and even sex by women during pregnancy or after menopause. These practices would be just as "unnatural" (and, presumably, just as bad) as gay sex. But there is no reason to accept these conclusions, because this whole line of reasoning is faulty. It rests on the assumption that *it is wrong to use parts of one's body for anything other than their natural purposes.* Why should we accept that assumption? The "purpose" of the eyes is to see; is it therefore wrong to use one's eyes for flirting or for giving a signal? The "purpose" of the fingers may be to grasp and poke; is it therefore wrong to snap one's fingers to get someone's attention? The idea that things should be used only in "natural" ways cannot be maintained, and so this version of the argument fails.

Third, because the word *unnatural* has a sinister sound, it might be understood simply as a term of evaluation. Perhaps it means something like "contrary to what a person ought to be." But if that is what "unnatural" means, then to say that homosexuality is wrong because it is unnatural would be vacuous. It would be like saying that homosexuality is wrong because it is wrong. That sort of empty remark provides no reason for condemning anything.

The idea that homosexuality is wrong because it's unnatural has great intuitive appeal for many people. Nevertheless, it seems to be an unsound argument. It fails on every interpretation.

But what of the claim that homosexuality is contrary to "family values"? James Dobson, founder of the conservative Christian group, "Focus on the Family," told his followers: "For more than 40 years, the homosexual activist movement has sought to implement a master plan that has had as its center-piece the utter destruction of the family." But how, exactly, are homosexuals trying to destroy the family? Gay activists want to make it easier for gays and lesbians to form families—they support same-sex marriage, domestic partner benefits, the right of gay couples to adopt children, and so on. Gay and lesbian activists find it ironic that the proponents of family values wish to deny them precisely these rights.

Perhaps this talk of "protecting family values" really amounts to saying, "Let's make sure we never have families *like that.*" But if so, then the question would remain: What is wrong with a family in which the children are raised by two mothers, or by two fathers? There is no evidence, scientific or otherwise, that this would be a bad thing. Meanwhile, gays continue to be disadvantaged under the current social arrangements. Homosexuals, like heterosexuals, often want children, but in Florida and Arkansas homosexuals are not allowed to adopt. Many gay people want to marry, but in America, gay marriage is legal only in Massachusetts and Connecticut. Moreover, 1,138 federal benefits are tied directly to marriage.

There is one other, specifically religious, argument that must be mentioned, namely, that homosexuality is condemned in the Bible. For example, Leviticus 18:22 says, "You may not lie with a man as with a woman; it is an abomination." Some commentators have said that, contrary to appearances, the Bible is really not so harsh toward homosexuality; and they explain how each relevant passage (there seem to be nine of them) should be understood. But suppose we accept that the Bible condemns homosexuality. What may we infer from this? Are we supposed to believe what the Bible says, simply because it says it?

This question will offend some people. To question the Bible, they believe, is to challenge the word of God. And this, they think, is an act of arrogance coming from creatures who should be showing gratitude to the Almighty. Questioning the Bible can also make people feel uncomfortable, since it may seem to challenge their whole way of life. However, thoughts like these cannot restrain our inquiry. Philosophy *is* about questioning whole ways of life. When the argument is given that homosexuality must be wrong because the Bible says so, this argument must be discussed on its own terms.

The problem with the argument is that, if we look at *other* things the Bible says, it does not appear to be a reliable guide to morality. Leviticus condemns homosexuality, but it also forbids eating sheep's fat (7:23), letting a woman into the church's sanctuary who has recently given birth (12:2–5), and seeing your uncle naked. The latter, like homosexuality, is deemed an abomination (18:14, 26). Even worse, Leviticus condemns to death those who curse their parents (20:9) and those who commit adultery (20:10). It says that a priest's daughter, if she "plays the whore," shall be burned alive (21:9), and it says that we may purchase slaves from nearby nations (25:44). In Exodus, it even says that it's okay to beat your slaves, so long as they don't die (21:20–21).

The point of all this is not to ridicule the Bible; the Bible, in fact, contains much that is true and wise. But we can conclude from examples like these that the Bible is not always right. And since it's not always right, we can't conclude that homosexuality is an abomination just because it says so in Leviticus.

At any rate, nothing can be morally right or wrong *simply* because an authority says so. If the precepts in a sacred text are not arbitrary, there must be some reason for them—we should be able to ask *why* the Bible condemns homosexuality and then to get an answer. That answer will then give the real explanation of why the thing is wrong.

But the main point here is not about homosexuality. The main point concerns the nature of moral thinking. Moral thinking and moral conduct are a matter of weighing reasons and being guided by them. But being guided by reason is very different from following one's feelings. When we have strong feelings, we may be tempted to ignore reason and go with the feelings. But in doing so, we would be opting out of moral thinking altogether. That is why, in focusing on attitudes and feelings, Ethical Subjectivism seems to be going in the wrong direction.

CHAPTER 4

Does Morality Depend on Religion?

The Good consists in always doing what God wills at any particular moment.

EMIL BRUNNER, *THE DIVINE IMPERATIVE* (1947)

I respect deities. I do not rely upon them.

MUSASHI MIYAMOTO, AT ICHIJOJI TEMPLE (ca. 1608)

4.1. The Presumed Connection between Morality and Religion

In 1995 the American Civil Liberties Union (ACLU) sued Judge Roy Moore of Gadsden, Alabama, for displaying the Ten Commandments in his courtroom. Such a display, it said, violates the separation of church and state. The ACLU may not have liked Moore, but Alabama voters did. In 2000, Moore successfully campaigned to become chief justice of the Alabama Supreme Court, running on a promise to "restore the moral foundation of law." Thus the "Ten Commandments judge" became the most powerful jurist in the state of Alabama.

Moore was not through making his point, however. In the wee hours of July 31, 2001, he had a granite monument to the Ten Commandments installed in the Alabama state judicial building. This monument weighed over five thousand pounds, and anyone entering the building could not miss it. Moore was sued again, but the people were behind him: 77% of Americans thought that he should be allowed to display his monument. Yet the law did not agree. When Moore disobeyed a court order to remove it, the Alabama Court of the Judiciary fired him, saying that he had placed himself above the law. Moore, how-ever, believed that he was putting *God* above the law.

The United States is a religious country. 78% of Ameri-cans say they believe in God, and another 15% say they believe in a universal spirit or higher power. Members of the clergy are often treated as moral experts in America: Hospitals ask them to sit on ethics committees; reporters interview them on the moral dimensions of a story; and churchgoers turn to them for counseling. The clergy even help decide whether movies will be rated "G," "PG," "PG-13," "R," or "NC-17." Priests and min-isters are assumed to be wise counselors who will give sound moral advice.

Why are the clergy regarded in this way? The reason is not that they have proven themselves to be better or wiser than other people—as a group, they seem to be neither better nor worse than the rest of us. There is a deeper reason why they are regarded as having special moral insight. In popular think-ing, morality and religion are inseparable: People commonly believe that morality can be understood only in the context of religion. So, because the clergy are authorities on religion, they are assumed to be authorities on morality as well.

It is not hard to see why people think this. When viewed from a nonreligious perspective, the universe seems to be a cold, meaningless place, devoid of value and purpose. In his essay "A Free Man's Worship," written in 1902, Bertrand Russell expressed what he called the "scientific" view of the world:

> That Man is the product of causes which had no prevision of the end they were achieving; that his origin, his growth, his hopes and fears, his loves and his beliefs, are but the outcome of accidental collocations of atoms; that no fire, no heroism, no intensity of thought and feeling, can preserve an individual life beyond the grave; that all the labours of the ages, all the devotion, all the inspiration, all the noonday brightness of human genius, are destined to extinction in the vast death of the solar system, and that the whole temple of Man's achievement must inevitably be buried beneath the debris of a universe in ruins—all these things, if not quite beyond dispute, are yet so nearly certain that no philosophy which rejects them can hope to stand.

From a religious perspective, however, things look very different. Judaism and Christianity teach that the world was created by a loving, all-powerful God to provide a home for us. We, in turn, were created in his image, to be his children. Thus, the world is not devoid of meaning and purpose. It is, instead, the arena in which God's plans and purposes are realized. What could be more natural, then, than to think of "morality" as part of religion, while the atheist's world has no place for values?

4.2. The Divine Command Theory

Christians, Jews, and Muslims all believe that God has told us to obey certain rules of conduct. God does not force these rules on us. He created us as free agents, so we may choose what to do. But if we live as we should, then we must follow God's laws. This idea has been expanded into a theory known as the Divine Command Theory. Essentially, it says that "morally right" is a matter of being commanded by God and "morally wrong" is a matter of being forbidden by God.

This theory has a number of attractive features. It immediately solves the old problem about the objectivity of ethics. Ethics is not merely a matter of personal feeling or social custom. Whether something is right or wrong is perfectly objective: It is right if God commands it and wrong if God forbids it. Moreover, the Divine Command Theory explains why anyone should bother with morality. Why not forget about "ethics" and just look out for yourself? If immorality is the violation of God's commandments, there is an easy answer: On the day of final reckoning, you will be held accountable.

There are, however, serious problems with the theory. Of course, atheists would not accept it, because they do not believe that God exists. But there are difficulties even for believers. The main problem was first noted by Plato, the Greek philosopher who lived 400 years before Jesus of Nazareth.

Plato wrote dialogues, or book-length conversations, that always featured his teacher Socrates. In one of them, the *Euthyphro,* there is a discussion of whether "right" can be defined as "that which the gods command." Socrates is skeptical and asks, Is conduct right because the gods command it, or do the gods command it because it is right? This is one of the most famous questions in the history of philosophy. The British philosopher

Antony Flew (1923–) suggests that "one good test of a person's aptitude for philosophy is to discover whether he can grasp [the] force and point" of this question.

Socrates' question is about whether God *makes* the moral truths true or whether he merely *recognizes* that they're true. There's a big difference between these options. I know that the Burj Dubai building in the United Arab Emirates is the tallest building in the world; I recognize that fact. However, I did not make it true. Rather, it was made true by the designers and builders in the city of Dubai. Is God's relation to ethics like my relation to the Burj Dubai building or like the relation of the builders? This question poses a dilemma, and either way out leads to trouble.

First, we might say that *right conduct is right because God commands it.* For example, according to Exodus 20:16, God commands us to be truthful. On this option, we should be truthful simply because God requires it. Apart from the divine command, truth telling is neither good nor bad. God's command makes truthfulness right, just as the builders of a skyscraper make the building tall. This is the Divine Command Theory. It is almost the theory of Shakespeare's character Hamlet. Hamlet said that nothing is good or bad, but thinking makes it so. According to the Divine Command Theory, nothing is good or bad, except when *God's* thinking makes it so.

But this idea encounters several difficulties.

1. *This conception of morality is mysterious.* What does it mean to say that God "makes" truthfulness right? It is easy enough to understand how physical objects are made, at least in principle. We have all made something, if only a sand castle or a peanut-butter-and-jelly sandwich. But making truthfulness right is not like that; it could not be done by rearranging things in our physical environment. How, then, could it be done? No one knows.

To see the problem, consider some wretched case of child abuse. On the theory we're now considering, God could make *that* instance of child abuse right—not by turning a slap into a friendly pinch of the cheek, but *by commanding that the slap is right.* This proposal defies human understanding. How could merely saying, or commanding, that the slap is right make it right? If true, this conception of morality would be a mystery.

2. *This conception of morality makes God's commands arbitrary.* We assume that God has good reasons for what he does. But suppose God commands truthfulness to be right. On this theory, he could have given different commands just as easily. He could have commanded us to be liars, and then lying, and not truthfulness, would be right. After all, before God issues his commands, no reasons for or against lying exist—*God is the one who creates the reasons.* And so, from a moral point of view, God's commands are arbitrary. This result may seem not only unacceptable but impious from a religious point of view.

3. *This conception of morality provides the wrong reasons for moral principles.* There are many things wrong with child abuse: It is malicious; it involves the unnecessary infliction of pain; it can have unwanted long-term psychological effects; and so on. However, the theory we're now considering cannot recognize any of these reasons as important. All it cares about, in the end, is whether child abuse runs counter to God's commands.

There are two ways of confirming that something is wrong here. First, notice something the theory implies: *If God didn't exist, child abuse wouldn't be wrong.* This is so because if God didn't exist, then God wouldn't be around to make child abuse wrong. However, child abuse would still be malicious, so it would still be wrong. Thus, the Divine Command Theory fails. Second, keep in mind that even a religious person might be genuinely in doubt as to what God has commanded. After all, religious texts disagree with each other, and sometimes there seem to be inconsistencies even within a single text. So, a person might be in doubt as to what God's will really is. However, a person needn't be in doubt as to whether child abuse is wrong. What God has commanded is one thing; what's wrong with hitting children is another.

There is a way to avoid these troublesome consequences. We can take the second of Socrates' options. We need not say that right conduct is right because God commands it. Instead, we may say that God commands us to do certain things *because they are right.* God, who is infinitely wise, recognizes that truthfulness is better than deceitfulness, and so he commands us to be truthful; he sees that killing is wrong, and so he commands us not to kill; and so on for all the moral rules.

If we take this option, we avoid the consequences that spoiled the first alternative. We needn't worry about how God makes it wrong to lie, since he doesn't. God's [...] not arbitrary; they are the result of his wisdom i [...] is best. Furthermore, we are not saddled with t[...] nations for our moral principles; rather, we ar[...] to whatever justifications of them seem appropriate.

Unfortunately, this second option leads to a different problem. In taking this option, we abandon the theological conception of right and wrong. When we say that God commands us to be truthful *because* truthfulness is right, we acknowledge a standard that is independent of God's will. The rightness exists prior to God's command and is the reason for the command. Thus, if we want to know why we should be truthful, the reply "because God commands it" does not really tell us. We may still ask, "*Why* does God command it?" and the answer to *that* question will provide the ultimate reason why truthfulness is good.

Many religious people believe that they must accept a theological conception of right and wrong because it would be sacrilegious not to do so. They feel, somehow, that if they believe in God, then right and wrong must be understood in terms of God's wishes. Our arguments, however, suggest that the Divine Command Theory is not only untenable but impious. And, in fact, some of the greatest theologians have rejected the theory for just this reason. Thinkers such as Saint Thomas Aquinas (1225–1274) connect morality with religion in a different way.

4.3. The Theory of Natural Law

In the history of Christian thought, the dominant theory of ethics is not the Divine Command Theory. That honor goes to the Theory of Natural Law. This theory has three main parts.

1. The Theory of Natural Law rests on a certain view of the world. On this view, the world has a rational order, with values and purposes built into its very nature. This conception derives from the Greeks, whose way of understanding the world dominated Western thinking for over 1700 years. The Greeks believed that *everything in nature has a purpose.*

Aristotle (384–322 B.C.) built this idea into his system of thought when he said that, in order to understand any thing, four questions must be asked: What is it? What is it made of? How did it come to exist? And what is it for? The answers might be: This is a knife; it is made of metal; it was made by a

.aftsman; and it is used for cutting. Aristotle assumed that the last question—What is it for?—could be asked of anything whatever. "Nature," he said, "belongs to the class of causes which act for the sake of something."

Obviously, artifacts such as knives have purposes, because craftsmen have built them with a purpose in mind. But what about natural objects that we do not make? Aristotle believed that they have purposes, too. One of his examples was that we have teeth so that we can chew. Biological examples are quite persuasive; each part of our bodies does seem, intuitively, to have a special purpose—eyes are for seeing, the heart is for pumping blood, and so on. But Aristotle's claim was not limited to organic beings. According to him, *everything* has a purpose. To take a different sort of example, he thought that rain falls so that plants can grow. He considered other alternatives, such as that the rain falls "of necessity" and that this helps the plants only "by coincidence," and rejected them.

The world, therefore, is an orderly, rational system, with each thing having its own proper place and serving its own special purpose. There is a neat hierarchy: The rain exists for the sake of the plants, the plants exist for the sake of the animals, and the animals exist—of course—for the sake of people. Aristotle says: "If then we are right in believing that nature makes nothing without some end in view, nothing to no purpose, it must be that nature has made all things specifically for the sake of man." This worldview is stunningly anthropocentric, or human-centered. Aristotle may be forgiven, however, when we consider that virtually every important thinker in our history has entertained some such thought. Humans are a remarkably vain species.

The Christian thinkers who came later found this worldview congenial. Only one thing was missing: God. Thus, the Christian thinkers said that the rain falls to help the plants *because that is what God intended,* and the animals are for human use because *that is what God made them for.* Values and purposes were thus conceived to be part of the divine plan.

2. A corollary of this way of thinking is that the "laws of nature" describe not only how things *are* but also how things *ought to be.* The world is in harmony when things serve their natural purposes. When they do not, or cannot, things have gone wrong. Eyes that cannot see are defective, and drought is a natural evil; the badness of both is explained by reference to natural law. But there are also implications for human conduct. Moral rules are now viewed as deriving from the laws of nature. Some ways of behaving are said to be "natural" while others are "unnatural"; and "unnatural" acts are said to be morally wrong.

Consider, for example, the duty of beneficence. We are morally required to care about our neighbors. Why? According to the Theory of Natural Law, beneficence is natural for us, given the kind of creatures we are. We are naturally social creatures who want and need the company of other people. Someone who does not care at all for others—who really does not care, through and through—is seen as deranged. Modern psychiatry says that such people suffer from *antisocial personality disorder*, and such people are commonly called *psychopaths* or *sociopaths*. A malicious personality is defective, just as eyes are defective if they cannot see. And, it may be added, this is true because we were created by God, with a specific "human" nature, as part of his overall plan.

The endorsement of beneficence is relatively uncontroversial. Natural-law theory has also been used, however, to support more contentious moral views. Religious thinkers often condemn "deviant" sexual practices, and they usually justify their condemnation by appealing to the Theory of Natural Law. If everything has a purpose, what is the purpose of sex? The obvious answer is procreation. Sexual activity that is not connected with making babies can therefore be viewed as "unnatural," and so such practices as masturbation and gay sex can be condemned for this reason. This way of thinking about sex dates back at least to Saint Augustine in the fourth century, and it is explicit in the writings of Saint Thomas Aquinas. The moral theology of the Catholic Church is based on natural-law theory.

Outside the Catholic Church, the Theory of Natural Law has few advocates today. It is generally rejected for three reasons.

First, the idea that "what's natural is good" seems open to obvious counterexamples. Sometimes what's natural is bad. People naturally care much more about themselves than they do about strangers, but this is regrettable. Disease occurs naturally, but disease is bad. Children are naturally self-centered, but parents don't think this is a good thing.

Second, the Theory of Natural Law seems to involve a confusion of "is" and "ought." In the 18th century, David Hume pointed out that *what is the case* and *what ought to be the case* are logically different notions, and no conclusion about one follows from the other. We can say that people are naturally disposed to be beneficent, but it does not follow that they *should* be beneficent. Similarly, it may be that sex does produce babies, but it does not follow that sex *ought* or *ought not* to be engaged in only for that purpose. Facts are one thing; values are another.

Third, the Theory of Natural Law is now widely rejected because its view of the world conflicts with modern science. The world as described by Galileo, Newton, and Darwin has no need for "facts" about right and wrong. Their explanations of natural phenomena make no reference to values or purposes. What happens just happens, due to the laws of cause and effect. If the rain benefits the plants, this is because the plants have evolved by the laws of natural selection in a rainy climate.

Thus, modern science gives us a picture of the world as a realm of facts, where the only "natural laws" are the laws of physics, chemistry, and biology, working blindly and without purpose. Whatever values may be, they are not part of the natural order. As for the idea that "nature has made all things specifically for the sake of man," that is only human vanity. To the extent that one accepts the worldview of modern science, one will be skeptical of the Theory of Natural Law. It is no accident that the theory was a product, not of modern thought, but of the Middle Ages.

3. The third part of the theory addresses the question of moral knowledge. How can we determine what is right and what is wrong? The Divine Command Theory says that we must consult God's commandments. The Theory of Natural Law gives a different answer. The "natural laws" that specify what we should do are laws of reason, which we are able to grasp because God has given us the power to understand them. Therefore, the Theory of Natural Law endorses the familiar idea that the right thing to do is whatever course of conduct has the best reasons on its side. To use the traditional terminology, moral judgments are "dictates of reason." As Saint Thomas Aquinas, the greatest natural-law theorist, wrote in his masterpiece the *Summa Theologica*, "To disparage the dictate of reason is equivalent to condemning the command of God."

This means that the religious believer has no special access to moral truth. The believer and the nonbeliever are in the same position. God has given both the same powers of reasoning; and so believer and nonbeliever alike may listen to reason and follow its directives. In an important sense, this leaves morality independent of religion. Religious belief does not affect the calculation of what is best, and the results of moral inquiry are religiously "neutral." Even though they may disagree about religion, believers and nonbelievers inhabit the same moral universe.

4.4. Religion and Particular Moral Issues

Some religious people will find the preceding discussion unsatisfying. It will seem too abstract to have any bearing on their actual moral lives. For them, the connection between morality and religion is an immediate, practical matter that centers on particular moral issues. It doesn't matter whether right and wrong are understood in terms of God's will or whether moral laws are laws of nature. What matters are the moral teachings of one's religion. The teachings of the Scriptures and the church are regarded as authoritative, determining the moral positions one must take. To mention only one example, many Christians think that they have no choice but to oppose abortion because it is condemned both by the church and (they assume) by the Scriptures.

Are there distinctively religious positions on major moral issues that believers must accept? The rhetoric of the pulpit suggests so. But there is good reason to think otherwise.

For one thing, it is often difficult to find specific moral guidance in the Scriptures. We face different problems than the Jews and the early Christians faced long ago; thus, it is not surprising that the Scriptures might be silent about moral issues that seem urgent to us. The Bible contains a number of general moral principles, for example, to love one's neighbor and to treat others as one would wish to be treated. Those principles are commendable, but they do not yield definite answers about what to do regarding the rights of workers, the extinction of species, the funding of medical research, and so on.

Another problem is that the Scriptures and church tradition are often ambiguous. Authorities disagree, leaving the believer in the awkward position of having to choose which element of the tradition to accept. For instance, the New Testament condemns being rich, and there is a long tradition of self-denial and charitable giving that affirms this teaching. But there is also an obscure Old Testament figure named Jabez who asked God to "enlarge my territories" (1 Chronicles 4:10), and God did. A recent book urging Christians to adopt Jabez as their model became a best-seller.

Thus, when people say that their moral views are derived from their religious commitments, they are often mistaken. In reality, something very different is going on. They are making up their minds about the moral issues and then interpreting the Scriptures, or church tradition, in a way that supports the moral conclusions they have already reached. Of course, this does not happen in every case, but it seems fair to say that it happens a lot. The question of riches is one example; abortion is another.

In the debate over abortion, religious issues are never far from the center of discussion. Religious conservatives hold that the fetus is a person from the moment of conception, and so aborting the fetus is a form of murder. They do not believe it should be the mother's choice whether to have an abortion, because that would be like saying she is free to commit murder.

The key premise in the conservative argument is that the fetus is a person from the moment of conception: not merely a *potential* person but an *actual* person with a full-fledged right to life. Liberals, of course, deny this—they say that the embryo is something less than that, at least during the early weeks of pregnancy.

The abortion debate is complex, but here we are concerned with just one small part of it. Conservatives sometimes say that, according to Christianity, fetal life is sacred. Is this the Christian view? To answer that question, one might look to the Scriptures or to church tradition.

The Scriptures. It is difficult to derive a prohibition against abortion from either the Jewish or the Christian Scriptures. Certain passages, however, are often quoted by conservatives because they seem to suggest that fetuses have full human status. One of the most frequently cited passages is from the first chapter of Jeremiah, in which Jeremiah quotes God as saying "Before I formed you in the womb I knew you, and before you were born I consecrated you." These words are presented as though they are God's endorsement of the conservative position: They are taken to mean that the unborn are "consecrated" to God.

In context, however, these words obviously mean something different. Suppose we read the whole passage in which they occur:

> Now the word of the Lord came to me, saying, "Before I formed you in the womb I knew you, and before you were born I consecrated you; I appointed you a prophet to the nations."
>
> Then I said, "Ah, Lord God! Behold, I do not know how to speak, for I am only a youth." But the Lord said to me,
>
> "Do not say, 'I am only a youth'; for to all to whom I send you, you shall go, and whatever I command you, you shall speak. Be not afraid of them, for I am with you to deliver you . . . ."

The sanctity of fetal life is not discussed in this passage. Instead, Jeremiah is asserting his authority as a prophet. He is saying, in effect, "God authorized me to speak for him; even though I resisted, he commanded me to speak." But Jeremiah puts the point more poetically; he has God saying that God had intended him to be a prophet even before he was born.

This often happens when the Scriptures are cited in connection with controversial moral issues. A few words are lifted from a passage that is concerned with something else entirely, and those words are then construed in a way that supports a favored moral position. When this happens, is it accurate to say that the person is "following the moral teachings of the Bible"? Or is it more accurate to say that he is searching the Scriptures to find support for a moral view he already believes, and then reading the desired conclusion into the Scriptures? If the latter, it suggests an arrogant attitude—the attitude that God himself must share one's own moral opinions!

Other biblical passages point more strongly to a liberal view of abortion. Three times the death penalty is recommended for women who have had sex out of wedlock, even though killing the woman would also kill her fetus (Genesis 38:24; Leviticus 21:9; Deuteronomy 22:20–21). This suggests that the fetus has no right to life. Also, in Exodus 21, God tells Moses that the penalty for murder is death; however, the penalty for causing a woman to miscarry is only a fine. The Law of Israel seemed to regard the fetus as something less than a person.

Church Tradition. Even if there is little scriptural basis for it, the contemporary church's stand is strongly anti-abortion. The typical churchgoer will hear ministers, priests, and bishops denouncing abortion in the strongest terms. It is no wonder, then, that many people feel that their religious commitment compels them to oppose abortion.

But it is worth noting that the church has not always taken this view. In fact, the idea that the fetus is a person "from the moment of conception" is a relatively new idea within the Christian church. Saint Thomas Aquinas accepted Aristotle's view that the soul is the "substantial form" of man. We need not discuss that technical doctrine, but it implies that one cannot have a human soul until one's body takes on a human shape. Aquinas knew that an embryo is not shaped like a human "from the moment of conception," and so he held that the embryo does not acquire a soul until several weeks into the pregnancy. This position was officially accepted by the church at the Council of Vienne in 1312.

However, in the 17th century, a curious view of fetal development came to be accepted, and this had unexpected consequences for the church's view of abortion. Peering through primitive microscopes at fertilized eggs, some scientists imagined that they saw tiny, perfectly formed people. They called the little person a "homunculus," and the idea took hold that from the very beginning the human embryo is a fully formed creature that needs only to get bigger and bigger until it is ready to be born.

If the embryo has a human shape from the moment of conception, then it follows, according to Aristotle and Aquinas, that it can have a soul from the very beginning. The church thus embraced the conservative view of abortion. The "homunculus," it said, is a person, and so we may not kill it.

However, as our understanding of human biology progressed, scientists began to realize that this view of fetal development was wrong. There is no homunculus; that was a mistake.

Today we know that Aquinas's original thought was right—embryos start out as a cluster of cells; "human form" comes later. But when the biological error was corrected, the church did not revert to its earlier moral position. Rather, it held fast to the conservative view of abortion, which it has espoused to this day.

The purpose of reviewing this history is not to suggest that the contemporary church's position is wrong. For all I have said, it may be right. My point is this: every generation reinterprets scripture to support its favored moral views. Abortion is but one example of this. We could also have discussed the church's shifting views on slavery, or the status of women, or capital punishment. In each case, people's moral convictions are not derived from their religion so much as superimposed on it.

The arguments in this chapter point to a common conclusion: Right and wrong are not to be understood in terms of God's will; morality is a matter of reason and conscience, not religious faith; and in any case, religious considerations do not provide definitive solutions to most of the moral problems that we face. Morality and religion are, in a word, different. In saying this, I do not deny that religious beliefs sometimes bear on moral issues. Consider, for example, the doctrine of eternal life. If some people go to heaven when they die—so that dying is a good thing for them—then this might affect the morality of killing these people. Or suppose we believe, upon studying ancient prophecies, that the world is about to end. This might diminish our fear of global warming. The relationship between morality and religion is complicated, but it is a relationship between two different subjects.

This conclusion may strike some readers as anti-religious. However, it has not been reached by questioning the validity of religion. The arguments we have considered do not assume that Christianity or any other theological system is false; they merely show that even if such a system is true, morality remains an independent matter.

CHAPTER 5

*E*thical Egoism

The achievement of his own happiness is man's highest moral purpose.

AYN RAND, *THE VIRTUE OF SELFISHNESS* (1961)

5.1. Is There a Duty to Help Starving People?

Each year millions of people die from health problems caused by malnutrition. Over 5,200 children under the age of five die every day from dehydration brought on by diarrhea. That comes to 1,900,000 children each year. If we add in the children who die from other preventable causes, the number increases to 9,700,000. Even if this estimate is too high, the number who die is staggering.

For those of us in the affluent countries, this poses an acute problem. We spend money on ourselves, not only on necessities but on luxuries—DVDs, jewelry, concert tickets, iPods, and so on. In America, even people with modest incomes enjoy such things. But we could forgo our luxuries and give the money for famine relief instead. The fact that we don't suggests that we regard our luxuries as more important than the lives of the starving.

Why do we let people starve when we could save them? Few of us actually believe our luxuries are that important. Most of us, if asked the question directly, would probably be a bit embarrassed, and we might say we should do more to help. We don't do more partly because we hardly ever think about the problem. Living our own comfortable lives, we are insulated from it. The starving people are dying at some distance from us; we do not see them, and we can avoid even thinking of them. When we do think of them, it is only abstractly, as statistics. Unfortunately for the hungry, statistics do not have much power to move us.

We respond differently when there is a "crisis," as when an earthquake struck China in 2008, killing thousands and leaving millions homeless. Then it is big news and relief efforts are mobilized. But when the needy are scattered, the situation does not seem so pressing. The 9.7 million children who die every year would probably be saved if they were all gathered in, say, Chicago.

But leaving aside the question of why we behave as we do, what is our duty? What *should* we do? Common sense might tell us to balance our own interests against the interests of others. It is understandable, of course, that we look out for ourselves, and no one can be blamed for attending to their own basic needs. But at the same time, the needs of others are important, and when we can help others—especially at little cost to ourselves—we should do so. So, if you have an extra $10, and giving it to a famine relief agency would help save the life of a child, then commonsense morality would say that you should do so.

This way of thinking assumes that we have duties to others simply because *they are people who could be helped or harmed by what we do.* If a certain action would benefit (or harm) other people, then that is a reason why we should (or should not) perform that action. The commonsense assumption is that other people's interests *count,* from a moral point of view.

But one person's common sense is another person's naïve platitude. Some people believe that we have no duties to other people. On their view, known as Ethical Egoism, each person ought to pursue his or her own self-interest exclusively. This is the morality of selfishness. It holds that our only duty is to do what is best for ourselves. Other people matter only insofar as they can benefit us.

5.2. Psychological Egoism

Before we discuss Ethical Egoism, we should discuss a theory it is often confused with—Psychological Egoism. Ethical Egoism claims that each person *ought* to pursue his or her own self-interest exclusively. Psychological Egoism, by contrast, asserts that each person *does in fact* pursue his or her own self-interest alone. Thus, these two theories are very different. It is one thing to say that people are self-interested and that our neighbors therefore will not give to charity. It is quite another thing to say that people *ought* to be self-interested and so our neighbors *ought* not to give to charity. Psychological Egoism makes a claim about human nature, or about the way things are; Ethical Egoism makes a claim about morality, or about the way things should be.

Psychological Egoism is not a theory of ethics; rather, it is a theory of human psychology. Nevertheless, moral philosophers have always been worried about it. If Psychological Egoism were true, this would seem to have devastating consequences for morality. If people are moved only by their own welfare, isn't it pointless to talk about what we "ought" to do? If we are just self-interested beings, then aren't we going to behave selfishly no matter what our well-meaning but naïve moral theories tell us to do?

Is Altruism Possible? Raoul Wallenberg, a Swedish businessman who could have stayed safely at home, spent the closing months of World War II in Budapest, Hungary. Wallenberg had volunteered to go there as part of Sweden's diplomatic mission after hearing reports of Hitler's "final solution to the Jewish problem." Once there, he helped persuade the Hungarian government to stop deporting Jews to the death camps. When the Hungarian government was replaced by a Nazi puppet regime, and the deportations resumed, Wallenberg issued "Swedish Protective Passes" to thousands of Jews, insisting that they all had connections with Sweden and were under the protection of his government. He helped many people find places to hide. When they were discovered, Wallenberg would stand between them and the Nazis, telling the Germans that they would have to shoot him first. At the end of the war, when there was chaos and other diplomats were fleeing, Wallenberg stayed behind. He is credited with saving as many as 15,000 lives. Wallenberg disappeared after the war, and for a long time no one knew what had happened. Now it is believed that he was killed, not by the Germans, but by the Soviets, who imprisoned him after taking over Hungary.

Wallenberg's story is more dramatic than most, but it is not unique. The Israeli government recognizes over 22,000 Gentiles who risked their lives trying to save Jews from being murdered in the Holocaust. The Israelis call these women and men, "The Righteous Among the Nations." And though few of us have saved lives, acts of altruism appear to be common. People do favors for one another. They give blood. They build homeless shelters. They volunteer in hospitals. They read to the blind. Many people give money to worthy causes. In some cases, the amount given is extraordinary. Warren Buffett, an American businessman, gave $37 billion to the Bill and Melinda Gates Foundation to promote global health and education. Zell Kravinsky, an American real estate investor, gave his entire $45-million fortune to charity. And then, for good measure, Kravinsky donated one of his kidneys to a complete stranger. Oseola McCarty, an 87-year-old African-American woman from Hattiesburg, Mississippi, gave $150,000 to endow a scholarship fund at the University of Southern Mississippi. For 75 years, she had saved up money, working as a maid. She never owned a car, and at the age of 87 she still walked over a mile to the nearest grocery store, pushing her own shopping cart.

These are remarkable deeds, but should they be taken at face value? According to Psychological Egoism, we may believe ourselves to be noble and self-sacrificing, but that is only an illusion. In reality, we care only for ourselves. Could this theory be true? Why have people believed it, in the face of so much evidence to the contrary? Two arguments are often given for Psychological Egoism.

The Argument That We Always Do What We Want to Do. If we describe one person's action as altruistic and another person's action as self-interested, we are overlooking the fact that in both cases *the person is merely doing what he or she most wants to do.* If Raoul Wallenberg chose to go to Hungary, and no one was coercing him, then he wanted to go there more than he wanted to remain in Sweden—and why should he be praised for altruism when he was only doing what he wanted to do? His action was dictated by his own desires, by his own sense of what he wanted. Thus, he was moved by his own self-interest. And since exactly the same may be said about any alleged act of kindness, we can conclude that Psychological Egoism must be true.

This argument, however, is flawed. There are things that we do, not because we want to, but because we feel that we *ought* to. For example, I may write my grandmother a letter because I promised my mother I would, even though I don't want to do it. It is sometimes suggested that we do such things because we most want to keep our promises. But that is not true. It is simply false to say that what I most want is to keep my promise to my mother. My strongest desire is to break my promise, but I keep it anyway, as a matter of conscience. For all we know, Wallenberg was in this position: Perhaps he wanted to stay in Sweden, but he felt that he had to go to Budapest to save lives. In any case, the fact that he chose to go does not imply that he most wanted to do so.

The argument has a second flaw. Suppose we concede that we always act on our strongest desires. Even if this were granted, it would not follow that Wallenberg acted out of self-interest. For if Wallenberg wanted to help others, even at great risk to himself, then that is precisely what makes his behavior contrary to Psychological Egoism. The mere fact that you act on your own desires does not mean that you are looking out for yourself; it all depends on *what* you desire. If you care only about your own welfare and give no thought to others, then you are acting out of self-interest; but if you want other people to be happy, and you act on that desire, then you are not. To put the point another way: In assessing whether an action is self-interested, the issue is not *whether* the action is based on a desire; the issue is *what kind of desire it is based on.* If what you want is to help someone else, then your motive is altruistic, not self-interested.

Therefore, this argument goes wrong in just about every way that an argument can go wrong: The premise is not true—we don't always do what we want to do—and even if it were true, the conclusion would not follow from it.

The Argument That We Always Do What Makes Us Feel Good. The second argument for Psychological Egoism appeals to the fact that so-called altruistic actions produce a sense of self-satisfaction in the person who performs them. Acting "unselfishly" makes people feel good about themselves, and that is the real point of it.

According to a 19th-century newspaper, this argument was made by Abraham Lincoln. The Springfield, Illinois, *Monitor* reported:

> Mr. Lincoln once remarked to a fellow-passenger on an old-time mud coach that all men were prompted by selfishness in doing good. His fellow-passenger was antagonizing this position when they were passing over a corduroy bridge that spanned a slough. As they crossed this bridge they espied an old razor-backed sow on the bank making a terrible noise because her pigs had got into the slough and were in danger of drowning. As the old coach began to climb the hill, Mr. Lincoln called out, "Driver, can't you stop just a moment?" Then Mr. Lincoln jumped out, ran back, and lifted the little pigs out of the mud and water and placed them on the bank. When he returned, his companion remarked: "Now, Abe, where does selfishness come in on this little episode?" "Why, bless your soul, Ed, that was the very essence of selfishness. I should have had no peace of mind all day had I gone on and left that suffering old sow worrying over those pigs. I did it to get peace of mind, don't you see?"

In this story, Honest Abe employs a time-honored tactic of Psychological Egoism: *the strategy of reinterpreting motives.* Everyone knows that people sometimes seem to act altruistically; but if we look deeper, we may find that something else is going on. And usually it is not hard to discover that the "unselfish" behavior is actually connected to some benefit for the person who does it. Thus, Lincoln talks about the peace of mind he got from rescuing the pigs.

Other examples of alleged altruism can also be reinterpreted. According to some of Raoul Wallenberg's friends, before traveling to Hungary, he was depressed and unhappy that his life wasn't amounting to much. So he undertook deeds that would make him a heroic figure. His quest for a more significant life was spectacularly successful—here we are, more than a half-century after his death, talking about him. Mother Teresa, the nun who spent her life working among the poor in Calcutta, is often cited as a perfect example of altruism—but, of course, she believed that she would be handsomely rewarded in heaven. And as for Zell Kravinsky, who gave away both his fortune and a kidney, his parents never gave him much praise, so he was always trying to do things that even they couldn't help but admire. Kravinsky himself said that, as he began to give away his money, he came to think of a donation as "a treat to myself. I really thought of it as something pleasurable."

Despite all this, Lincoln's argument is badly flawed. It may be true that one of Lincoln's motives in saving the pigs was to preserve his own peace of mind. *But the fact that Lincoln had a self-interested motive doesn't mean that he didn't have benevolent motives as well.* In fact, Lincoln's desire to help the pigs might have been even greater than his desire to preserve his own peace of mind. And if this isn't true in Lincoln's case, it will be true in other cases: If I see a child drowning, my desire to help that child will usually be greater than my desire to avoid a guilty conscience. Cases like these are counterexamples to Psychological Egoism.

In some instances of altruism, we may not have *any* self-interested motives. In 2007, a 50-year-old construction worker named Wesley Autrey was waiting for a subway train in New York City. Autrey saw a man near him collapse, his body convulsing. The man got up, only to stumble to the edge of the platform and fall onto the train tracks. At that moment, the headlights of a train appeared. "I had to make a split decision," Autrey later said. He then leapt onto the tracks and lay on top of the man, pressing him down into a space a foot deep. The train's brakes screeched, but it could not stop in time. People on the platform screamed. Five cars passed over the men, smudging Autrey's blue knit cap with grease. When onlookers realized that both men were safe, they broke out into applause. "I just saw someone who needed help," Autrey later said. He had saved the man's life, never giving a thought to his own well-being.

There is a general lesson to be learned here, having to do with the nature of desire. We want all sorts of things—money, friends, fame, a new car, and so on—and because we desire these things, we may derive satisfaction from getting them. But the object of our desire is not usually the feeling of satisfaction—typically, that is not what we are after. What we are after is simply the money, the friends, the fame, and the car. It is the same with helping others. Our desire to help others often comes first; the good feelings we may get are merely a by-product.

Conclusion about Psychological Egoism. If Psychological Egoism is so implausible, why have intelligent people been attracted to it? Some people like the theory's cynical view of human nature; Psychological Egoism provides a response to human vanity. People may also like its simplicity. It would be pleasing to find a single formula that explains all human behavior. And since self-regard is a tremendously important factor in motivation, it is natural to try to use it to account for all human action. However, every attempt to do so seems strained and implausible; Psychological Egoism is not a credible theory.

Thus, morality has nothing to fear from Psychological Egoism. Since we *can* be moved by regard for others, it is not pointless to talk about whether we *should* care about our neighbors. Moral theorizing need not be a naïve endeavor, based on an unrealistic view of human nature.

5.3. Three Arguments for Ethical Egoism

Ethical Egoism, again, is the doctrine that each person ought to pursue his or her own self-interest exclusively. This is not the commonsense idea that one should promote one's own interests *in addition to* the interests of others. Ethical Egoism is the radical idea that the principle of self-interest accounts for *all* of one's obligations.

However, Ethical Egoism does not say that you should *avoid* actions that help others. Sometimes your interests will coincide with the interests of others, so by helping yourself you'll help them too. For example, if you can convince your teacher to cancel the assignment, this will benefit you *and* your classmates. Ethical Egoism does not forbid such actions; in fact, it may recommend them. The theory insists only that in such cases the benefit to others is not what makes the act right. Rather, the act is right because it is to your own advantage.

Nor does Ethical Egoism imply that in pursuing one's interests, one should always do what one wants to do, or what gives one the most pleasure in the short run. Someone may want to smoke cigarettes, or bet all his money at the racetrack, or set up a meth lab in his basement. Ethical Egoism would frown on all this, despite the short-term benefits. Ethical Egoism says that a person ought to do what really is in his or her own best interests, over the long run. It endorses selfishness, not foolishness.

Now let's discuss the three main arguments for Ethical Egoism.

The Argument That Altruism Is Self-Defeating. The first argument has several variations, each suggesting the same general point:

- Each of us is intimately familiar with our own individual wants and needs. Moreover, each of us is uniquely placed to pursue those wants and needs effectively. At the same time, we know the desires and needs of other people only imperfectly, and we are not well situated to pursue them. Therefore, it is reasonable to believe that if we set out to be "our brother's keeper," we will often bungle the job and end up doing more harm than good.
- At the same time, the policy of "looking out for others" is an offensive intrusion into other people's privacy; it is essentially a policy of minding other people's business.
- Making other people the object of one's "charity" is degrading to them; it robs them of their dignity and self-respect. The offer of charity says, in effect, that they are not competent to care for themselves; and the statement is self-fulfilling. They cease to be self-reliant and become passively dependent on others. That is why the recipients of "charity" are often resentful rather than appreciative.

Thus, the policy of "looking out for others" is said to be self-defeating. If we want to do what is best for people, we should not adopt so-called altruistic policies. On the contrary, if each person looks after his or her own interests, everyone will be better off.

It is possible to object to this argument on a number of grounds. Of course, no one favors bungling, butting in, or depriving people of their self-respect. But is that really what we are doing when we feed hungry children? Is the starving child in Ethiopia really harmed when we "intrude" into "her business" by supplying food? It hardly seems likely. Yet we can set this point aside, for considered as an argument for Ethical Egoism, this way of thinking has an even more serious defect.

The trouble is that it isn't really an argument for Ethical Egoism at all. The argument concludes that we should adopt certain policies of behavior, and on the surface, they appear to be egoistic policies. However, the *reason* we should adopt those policies is decidedly unegoistic. It is said that adopting those policies will promote the betterment of society—but according to Ethical Egoism, that is not something we should care about. Spelled out fully, the argument says:

(1) We ought to do whatever will best promote everyone's interests.

(2) The best way to promote everyone's interests is for each of us to pursue our own interests exclusively.

(3) Therefore, each of us should pursue our own interests exclusively.

If we accept this reasoning, then we are not Ethical Egoists. Even though we might end up behaving like egoists, our ultimate principle is one of beneficence—we are doing what we think will help everyone, not merely what we think will benefit ourselves. Rather than being egoists, we turn out to be altruists with a peculiar view of what promotes the general welfare.

Ayn Rand's Argument. Ayn Rand (1905–1982) is not read much by philosophers. The ideas associated with her name—that capitalism is a morally superior economic system and that morality demands absolute respect for the rights of individuals—are developed more rigorously by other writers. Nevertheless, she was a charismatic figure who attracted a devoted following during her lifetime. Today, more than a quarter-century after her death, the Ayn Rand industry is still going strong. Ethical Egoism is associated with her more than with any other 20th-century writer.

Ayn Rand regarded the "ethics of altruism" as a totally destructive idea, both in society as a whole and in the lives of individuals taken in by it. Altruism, to her way of thinking, leads to a denial of the value of the individual. It says to a person: Your life is merely something that may be sacrificed. "If a man accepts the ethics of altruism," she writes, "his first concern is not how to live his life, but how to sacrifice it." Those who promote the ethics of altruism are beneath contempt—they are parasites who, rather than working to build and sustain their own lives, leech off those who do. Rand continues:

> Parasites, moochers, looters, brutes and thugs can be of no value to a human being—nor can he gain any benefit from living in a society geared to *their* needs, demands and protections, a society that treats him as a sacrificial animal

and penalizes him for his virtues in order to reward *them* for their vices, which means: a society based on the ethics of altruism.

By "sacrificing one's life," Rand does not mean anything so dramatic as dying. A person's life consists, in part, of projects undertaken and goods earned and created. Thus, to demand that a person abandon his projects or give up his goods is to demand that he "sacrifice his life."

Rand also suggests that there is a metaphysical basis for Ethical Egoism. Somehow, it is the only ethic that takes seriously the *reality* of the individual person. She bemoans "the enormity of the extent to which altruism erodes men's capacity to grasp . . . the value of an individual life; it reveals a mind from which the reality of a human being has been wiped out."

What, then, of the hungry children? It might be said that Ethical Egoism itself "reveals a mind from which the reality of a human being has been wiped out," namely, the human being who is starving. But Rand quotes with approval the answer given by one of her followers: "Once, when Barbara Brandon was asked by a student: 'What will happen to the poor . . . ?' she answered: 'If *you* want to help them, you will not be stopped.'"

All these remarks are part of one continuous argument that can be summarized like this:

(1) Each person has only one life to live. If we value the individual, then we must agree that this life is of supreme importance. After all, it is all one has, and all one is.

(2) The ethics of altruism regards the life of the individual as something one must be ready to sacrifice for the good of others. Therefore, the ethics of altruism does not take seriously the value of the individual.

(3) Ethical Egoism, which allows each person to view his or her own life as being of ultimate value, does take the individual seriously—it is, in fact, the only philosophy that does.

(4) Thus, Ethical Egoism is the philosophy that we ought to accept.

One problem with this argument, as you may have noticed, is that it assumes we have only two choices: Either we accept the ethics of altruism, or we accept Ethical Egoism. The choice is then made to look obvious by depicting the ethics of altruism as an insane doctrine that only an idiot would accept. The ethics of altruism is said to be the view that one's own interests have *no* value and that one must be ready to sacrifice oneself *totally* any time *anybody* asks it. If this is the alternative, then any other view, including Ethical Egoism, will look good by comparison.

But that is hardly a fair picture of the choices. What we called the commonsense view stands between the two extremes. It says that one's own interests and the interests of others are *both* important, and must be balanced against each other. Sometimes, one should act in the interests of others; other times, one should take care of oneself. So, even if we should reject the extreme ethics of altruism, it does not follow that we must accept the other extreme of Ethical Egoism. There is a middle ground.

Ethical Egoism as Compatible with Commonsense Morality. The third line of reasoning takes a different approach. Ethical Egoism is usually presented as a *revisionist* moral philosophy, that is, as a philosophy that says our commonsense moral views are mistaken. It is possible, however, to interpret Ethical Egoism as a theory that accepts commonsense morality.

This interpretation goes as follows: Ordinary morality consists in obeying certain rules. We must speak the truth, keep our promises, avoid harming others, and so on. At first glance, these duties appear to have little in common—they are just a bunch of discrete rules. Yet there may be some hidden unity underlying the hodgepodge of separate duties. Ethical Egoists would say that all these duties are ultimately derived from the one fundamental principle of self-interest.

Understood in this way, Ethical Egoism is not such a radical doctrine. It does not challenge commonsense morality; it only tries to explain and systematize it. And it does a surprisingly good job. It can provide plausible explanations of the duties mentioned above, and more:

- *The duty not to harm others:* If we do things that harm other people, other people will not mind doing things that harm us. We will be shunned and despised; others will not have us as friends and will not do us favors when we need them. If our offenses against others are serious enough, we may end up in jail. Thus, it is to our own advantage to avoid harming others.

- *The duty not to lie:* If we lie to other people, we will suffer all the ill effects of a bad reputation. People will distrust us and avoid doing business with us. We need people to be honest with us, but they won't be unless we are honest with them. Thus, it is to our own advantage to be truthful.
- *The duty to keep our promises:* It is to our own advantage to enter into mutually beneficial arrangements with other people. To benefit from those arrangements, we need to be able to rely on others to keep their word. But we can hardly expect them to do that if we do not keep our promises to them. Therefore, from the point of view of self-interest, we should keep our promises.

Pursuing this line of reasoning, Thomas Hobbes (1588–1679) suggested that the principle of Ethical Egoism leads to nothing less than the Golden Rule: We should "do unto others" because if we do, others will be more likely to "do unto us."

Does this argument succeed in establishing Ethical Egoism as a viable theory of morality? It is, in my opinion at least, the best try. But there are two serious problems with it. First, the argument does not prove as much as it needs to. It shows only that it is *mostly* to one's advantage to avoid harming others. A situation might arise in which you could profit from doing something horrible, like killing someone. In such a case, Ethical Egoism cannot explain why you shouldn't do the horrible thing. Thus, it looks like some of our moral obligations cannot be derived from self-interest.

Second, suppose it is true that contributing money for famine relief is somehow to one's own advantage. It doesn't follow that this is the *only* reason to do so. Another reason might be *to help the starving people.* Ethical Egoism says that self-interest is the only reason why we should help others, but nothing in the present argument really supports that.

5.4. Three Arguments against Ethical Egoism

The Argument That Ethical Egoism Endorses Wickedness. Consider these wicked actions, taken from various newspaper stories: To make more money, a pharmacist filled prescriptions for cancer patients using watered-down drugs. A paramedic gave emergency patients injections of sterile water rather than morphine, so he could sell the morphine. Parents fed a baby acid so they could fake a lawsuit, claiming the baby's formula was tainted. A nurse raped two patients while they were unconscious. A 73-year-old man kept his daughter locked in a cellar for 24 years and fathered seven children with her, against her will. A 60-year-old man shot his letter carrier seven times because he was $90,000 in debt and thought that being in federal prison would be better than being homeless.

Suppose that someone could actually benefit by doing such things. Wouldn't Ethical Egoism have to approve of such actions? This seems like enough to discredit the doctrine. However, this objection might be unfair to Ethical Egoism, because in saying that these actions are wicked, we are appealing to a nonegoistic conception of wickedness. Thus, some philosophers have tried to show that there are deeper logical problems with Ethical Egoism. The following argument is typical of the refutations they have proposed.

The Argument That Ethical Egoism Is Logically Inconsistent. In his book *The Moral Point of View* (1958), Kurt Baier argues that Ethical Egoism cannot be correct, on purely logical grounds. Baier thinks that the theory leads to contradictions. If this is true, then Ethical Egoism is indeed mistaken, for no theory can be true if it is self-contradictory.

Suppose, Baier says, two people are running for president. Let's call them "D" and "R," to stand for "Democrat" and "Republican." Since it would be in D's interest to win, it would be in D's interest to kill R. From this it follows, on Ethical Egoism, that D ought to kill R—it is D's moral duty to do so. But it is also true that it is in R's interest to stay alive. From this it follows that R ought to stop D from killing her—that is R's duty. Now here's the problem. When R protects herself from D, her act is both wrong and not wrong—wrong because it prevents D from doing his duty, and not wrong because it is in R's best interests. But one and the same act cannot be both morally wrong and not morally wrong.

Does this argument refute Ethical Egoism? At first glance, it seems persuasive. However, it is complicated, so we need to set it out with each step individually identified. Then we will be in a better position to evaluate it. Spelled out fully, it looks like this:

(1) Suppose it is each person's duty to do what is in his own best interest.

(2) It is in D's best interest to kill R, so D will win the election.

(3) It is in R's best interest to prevent D from killing her.

(4) Therefore, D's duty is to kill R, and R's duty is to prevent D from doing it.

(5) But it is wrong to prevent someone from doing his duty.

(6) Therefore, it is wrong for R to prevent D from killing her.

(7) Therefore, it is wrong and not wrong for R to prevent D from killing her.

(8) But no act can be wrong and not wrong; that is a self-contradiction.

(9) Therefore, the assumption with which we started—that it is each person's duty to do what is in his own best interest—cannot be true.

When the argument is set out in this way, we can see its hidden flaw. The logical contradiction—that it is wrong and not wrong for R to prevent D from killing her—does not follow simply from the principle of Ethical Egoism as stated in step (1). It follows from that principle *together with* the premise expressed in step (5), namely, that "it is wrong to prevent someone from doing his duty." By putting step (5) in the argument, Baier has added his own assumption.

Thus, we need not reject Ethical Egoism. Instead, we could simply reject this additional premise and thereby avoid the contradiction. That is surely what the Ethical Egoist would do, for the Ethical Egoist would never say, without qualification, that it is always wrong to prevent someone from doing his duty. He would say, instead, that whether one ought to prevent someone from doing his duty depends entirely on whether it would be to one's own advantage to do so. Regardless of whether we think this is a correct view, it is at least what the

Ethical Egoist would say. And so, this attempt to convict the egoist of self-contradiction fails.

The Argument That Ethical Egoism Is Unacceptably Arbitrary.
Now we come to the argument that I think comes closest to an outright refutation of Ethical Egoism. It is also the most interesting of the arguments, because it provides some insight into why the interests of other people *should* matter to us. But before presenting this argument, we need to look at a general point about moral values.

There is a whole family of moral views that have this in common: They divide people into groups and say that the interests of some groups count more than the interests of other groups. Racism is the most conspicuous example. Racism divides people into groups according to race and assigns greater importance to the interests of one race than to the interests of other races. All forms of discrimination work this way: anti-Semitism, nationalism, sexism, ageism, and so on. People in the grip of such views will think, in effect, "*My* race counts for more," or "Those who believe in *my* religion count for more," or "*My* country counts for more," and so on.

Can such views be defended? The people who accept such views don't usually care to give arguments—racists, for example, rarely try to offer a rational justification for racism. But suppose they did. What could they say?

There is a general principle that stands in the way of any such justification. Let's call it the Principle of Equal Treatment: *We should treat people in the same way unless there is a relevant difference between them.* For example, suppose we're considering whether to admit two students to law school. If both students graduated from college with honors and aced the entrance exam—if both are equally qualified—then it is merely arbitrary to admit one but not the other. However, if one graduated with honors and scored well on the admissions test while the other dropped out of college and never took the test, then it is acceptable to admit the first student but not the second.

Two points should be made about this principle. The first is that treating people in the same way does not always mean ensuring the same outcome for them. During the Vietnam War, young American men desperately wanted to avoid getting drafted into the armed services, and the government had to decide the order in which draft boards would call people up. In 1969, the first "draft lottery" was televised to a national audience. Here is how it worked: The days of the year were written on 366 slips of paper (one slip for February 29) and inserted into blue plastic capsules. Those capsules were placed in a glass jar and mixed up. Then, one by one, the capsules were drawn. The first was for September 14—young men with that birthday, age 18–26, would be drafted first. The winners of the lottery, drawn last, were born on June 8. These young men never got drafted. In college dormitories, groups of students watched the drawings live, and it was easy to tell whose birthday had just come up—whoever just shouted out or swore. Obviously, the outcomes were different: In the end, some people got drafted and others didn't. However, the process was fair. By giving everyone an equal chance in the lottery, the government treated everyone in the same way.

A second point concerns the scope of the principle, or its range of application. Suppose you're not going to use your ticket to the big game, so you give it to a friend. In doing so, you are treating your friend better than everyone else you could have given the ticket to. Does your action violate the Principle of Equal Treatment? Does it need justification? Moral philosophers disagree on this question. Some think that the principle does not apply to cases like this. The principle applies only in "moral contexts," and what you should do with your ticket is not important enough to count as a moral question. Others think that your action does require justification, and various justifications might be offered. Your action might be justified by the nature of friendship; or by the fact that it would be impossible for you to hold a lottery at the last minute for all the ticketless fans; or by the fact that you own the ticket, so you can do what you want with it. It doesn't matter, from our point of view, who is right about the scope of the principle. Suffice it to say that everyone accepts the Principle of Equal Treatment, in one form or another.

Let's now apply that principle to racism. Can a racist point to any differences between, say, white people and black people that would justify treating them differently? In the past, racists have sometimes tried to do this by portraying blacks as lazy, unintelligent, and threatening. In doing so, the racists show that even they accept the Principle of Equal Treatment—the point of the stereotypes is to supply the "relevant differences" needed to justify differences in treatment. If such accusations were true, then differential treatment would be justified in some circumstances. But, of course, they are not true; there are no such differences between the races. Thus, racism is an arbitrary doctrine—it advocates treating people differently even though there are no differences between them to justify it.

Ethical Egoism is a moral theory of the same type. It advocates that each of us divide the world into two categories of people—ourselves and everyone else—and that we regard the interests of those in the first group as more important than the interests of those in the second group. But each of us can ask, What is the difference between me and everyone else that justifies placing myself in this special category? Am I more intelligent? Are my accomplishments greater? Do I enjoy life more? Are my needs or abilities different from the needs or abilities of others? In short, *what makes me so special?* Failing an answer, it turns out that Ethical Egoism is an arbitrary doctrine, in the same way that racism is arbitrary. Both doctrines violate the Principle of Equal Treatment.

Thus, we should care about the interests of other people because their needs and desires are comparable to our own. Consider, one last time, the starving children we could feed by giving up some of our luxuries. Why should we care about them? We care about ourselves, of course—if we were starving, we would do almost anything to get food. But what is the difference between us and them? Does hunger affect them any less? Are they less deserving than we are? If we can find no relevant difference between us and them, then we must admit that, if our needs should be met, then so should theirs. This realization—that we are on a par with one another—is the deepest reason why our morality must recognize the needs of others. And that is why, ultimately, Ethical Egoism fails as a moral theory.

CHAPTER 6

The Idea of a Social Contract

The passions that incline men to peace are fear of death, desire of such things as are necessary [for comfortable] living, and a hope by their industry to obtain them. And reason suggests convenient articles of peace, upon which men may be drawn to agreement. These articles . . . are called the Laws of Nature.

THOMAS HOBBES, *LEVIATHAN* (1651)

6.1. Hobbes's Argument

Suppose we take away all the traditional props for morality. Assume, first, that there is no God to make commands and reward virtue. Next, suppose that no "natural purposes" are built into the nature of things. Finally, assume that human beings are naturally selfish—people are essentially motivated to pursue their own interests. Where, then, does morality come from? If we cannot appeal to God, natural purpose, or altruism, is there anything left to base morality on?

Thomas Hobbes, the foremost British philosopher of the 17th century, tried to show that morality does not depend on any of those things. Instead, morality should be understood as the solution to a practical problem that arises for self-interested human beings. We all want to live as well as possible; but in order to flourish, we need a peaceful, cooperative social order. And we cannot have one without rules. The moral rules are simply the rules that we need in order to get the benefits of social living. That—not God, inherent purposes, or altruism—is the key to understanding ethics.

Hobbes begins by asking what it would be like if there were no way to enforce social rules. Suppose there were no government institutions—no laws, no police, and no courts. In this situation, each of us would be free to do as we pleased. Hobbes called this "the state of nature." What would it be like?

Hobbes thought it would be dreadful. In *Leviathan,* he writes that there would be

> no place for industry, because the fruit thereof is uncertain: and consequently no culture of the earth; no navigation, nor use of the commodities that may be imported by sea; no commodious building; no instruments of moving, and removing, such things as require much force; no knowledge of the face of the earth; no account of time; no arts; no letters; no society; and which is worst of all, continual fear, and danger of violent death; and the life of man, solitary, poor, nasty, brutish, and short.

The state of nature would be awful, Hobbes thought, due to four basic facts about human life:

- There is *equality of need.* Each of us needs the same basic things in order to survive—food, clothing, shelter, and so on. Although we may differ in some of our needs (diabetics need insulin, others don't), we are all essentially alike.
- There is *scarcity.* We do not live in the Garden of Eden, where milk flows in streams and every tree hangs heavy with fruit. The world is a hard, inhospitable place, where the things we need do not exist in abundance. We have to work hard to produce them, and even then they may be in short supply.
- There is *the essential equality of human power.* Who will get the scarce goods? No one is so superior to others in strength and cunning that she can simply take what she wants. Some people are smarter and tougher than others, but even the strongest can be brought down by others acting together.
- Finally, there is *limited altruism.* If we cannot prevail by our own strength, what hope do we have? Can we rely on the goodwill of others? We cannot. Even if people are not wholly selfish, they care most about themselves, and we cannot assume that they will step aside when their interests conflict with ours.

When we put these facts together, a grim picture emerges. We all need the same basic things, and there aren't enough of them to go around. Therefore, we will have to compete for them. But no one has what it takes to prevail in this competition, and no one—or almost no one—will look after the needs of his neighbor. The result, as Hobbes puts it, is a "constant state of war, of one with all." And it is a war no one can win. Anyone who wants to survive will try to seize what he needs and prepare to defend it from attack. Meanwhile, others will be doing the same thing. Life in the state of nature would be intolerable.

Hobbes did not think this was mere speculation. He pointed out that this is what actually happens when governments collapse, for example, during a civil uprising. People hoard food, arm themselves, and lock out their neighbors. Moreover, nations themselves behave like this when international law is weak. Without a strong, overarching authority to maintain the peace, countries guard their borders, build up their armies, and feed their own people first.

To escape the state of nature, we must find a way to work together. In a stable and cooperative society, we can produce more essential goods and distribute them in a rational way. But establishing such a society is not easy. People must agree on rules to govern their interactions. They must agree, for example, not to harm one another and not to break their promises.

Hobbes calls such an agreement "the social contract." As a society, we follow certain rules, and we have ways to enforce them. Some of those ways involve the law—if you assault someone, the police may arrest you. Other ways involve "the court of public opinion"—if you get a reputation for lying, then people may turn their backs on you. All of these rules, taken together, form the social contract.

It is only within the context of the social contract that we can become beneficent beings, because the contract creates the conditions under which we can afford to care about others. In the state of nature, it is every man for himself; it would be foolish for anyone to look out for others and put his own interests in jeopardy. But in society, altruism becomes possible. By releasing us from "the continual fear of violent death," the social contract frees us to take heed of others. Jean-Jacques Rousseau (1712–1778) went so far as to say that we become *different kinds of creatures* when we enter civilized relations with others. In *The Social Contract* (1762), he writes:

> The passage from the state of nature to the civil state produces a very remarkable change in man.... Then only, when the voice of duty takes the place of physical impulses . . . does man, who so far had considered only himself, find that he is forced to act on different principles, and to consult his reason before listening to his inclinations. . . . His faculties are so stimulated and developed, . . . his feelings so ennobled, and his whole soul so uplifted, that, did not the abuses of this new condition often degrade him below that which he left, he would be bound to bless continually the happy moment which took him from it forever, and, instead of a stupid and unimaginative animal, made him an intelligent being and a man.

And what does the "voice of duty" require this new man to do? It requires him to set aside his self-centered designs in favor of rules that benefit everyone. But he is able to do this only because others have agreed to do the same thing—that is the essence of the "contract."

The Social Contract Theory explains both the purpose of morality and the purpose of the state. The moral rules make social living possible, and the state exists to enforce the most important of those rules. We can summarize the social contract conception of morality as follows: *Morality consists in the set of rules, governing behavior, that rational people will accept, on the condition that others accept them as well.*

6.2. The Prisoner's Dilemma

Hobbes's argument is one way of arriving at the Social Contract Theory. Another line of thought has also impressed philosophers in recent years. It stems from a problem known as the Prisoner's Dilemma, first formulated around 1950 by the social scientists Merrill M. Flood and Melvin Dresher. Here's how it goes.

Suppose you live in a totalitarian society, and one day, to your astonishment, you are arrested and charged with treason. The police say that you have been plotting against the government with a man named Smith, who has also been arrested and is being held in a separate cell. The interrogator demands that you confess. You protest your innocence; you don't even know

Smith. But this does no good. It soon becomes clear that your captors are not interested in the truth; they merely want to convict someone. They offer you the following deal:

- If Smith does not confess, but you confess and testify against him, they will release you. You will go free, whereas Smith, who did not cooperate, will be put away for 10 years.
- If Smith confesses and you do not, the situation will be reversed—he will go free while you get 10 years.
- If you both confess, you will each be sentenced to 5 years.
- If neither of you confesses, there won't be enough evidence to convict either of you. They can hold you for a year, but then they will have to let both of you go.

Finally, you are told that Smith is being offered the same deal; but you cannot communicate with him, and you have no way of knowing what he will do.

The problem is this: Assuming that your only goal is to spend as little time in jail as possible, what should you do? Confess or not confess? For the purposes of this problem, you should forget about maintaining your dignity, standing up for your rights, and other such notions. That is not what this problem is about. You should also forget about trying to help Smith. This problem is strictly about calculating what is in your own best interests. What will get you free the quickest?

At first glance, it may seem that the question cannot be answered unless you know what Smith will do. But that is an illusion. The problem has a perfectly clear solution: No matter what Smith does, you should confess. This can be shown by the following reasoning:

(1) Either Smith will confess or he won't.

(2) Suppose Smith confesses. Then, if you confess you will get 5 years, whereas if you do not confess you will get 10 years. Therefore, if he confesses, you are better off confessing.

(3) On the other hand, suppose Smith does not confess. Then, if you confess you will go free, whereas if you do not confess you get one year. Therefore, if Smith does not confess, you will still be better off confessing.

(4) Therefore, you should confess. That will get you out
of jail the soonest, no matter what Smith does.

So far, so good. But remember that Smith is being offered the
same deal. Thus, he will also confess. The result will be that you
both get 5-year sentences. *But if you had both done the opposite,
you both could have gotten out in only one year.* It's a curious situation: Since you and Smith both act selfishly, you both wind up
worse off.

Now suppose you can communicate with Smith. In that
case, you could make a deal with him. You could agree that
neither of you will confess; then you will both get the 1-year
detention. By cooperating, you will both be better off than if
you act independently. Cooperating will not get either of you
the optimum result—immediate freedom—but it will get both
of you a better result than you would get going it alone.

It is vital, however, that any agreement between you and
Smith be enforceable, because if he reneges and confesses while
you keep the bargain, you will end up serving the maximum
10 years while he goes free. Thus, in order for you to rationally
participate in such a deal, you need to be sure that he will keep
up his end. Only an enforceable agreement provides a way out
of the dilemma.

Morality as the Solution to Prisoner's-Dilemma-Type Problems.
The Prisoner's Dilemma is not just a clever puzzle. Although
the story we have told is fictitious, the pattern it exemplifies
comes up often in real life. Consider, for example, the choice
between two general strategies of living. You could pursue your
own self-interests exclusively—in every situation, you could
do whatever will benefit yourself, taking no notice of anyone
else. Let us call this "acting selfishly." Alternatively, you could
be concerned with other people's welfare as well as your own,
balancing the two against each other, and sometimes forgoing
your own interests in order to benefit others. Let us call this
strategy "acting benevolently."

But it is not only you who has to decide how to live. Other
people also have to choose which strategy to adopt. There are
four possibilities: (a) You could be selfish while other people
are benevolent; (b) others could be selfish while you are benevolent; (c) everyone could be selfish; and (d) everyone could

be benevolent. How would you fare in each of these situations? Purely from the standpoint of your own welfare, you might assess the possibilities like this:

- You would be best off if you were selfish while other people were benevolent. You would get the benefit of their generosity without having to return the favor. (In this situation, you would be a "free rider.")
- Second-best would be the situation in which everyone was benevolent. You would no longer have the advantages that come from ignoring other people's interests, but you would be treated well by others. (This is the situation of "ordinary morality.")
- A bad situation, but not the worst, would be one in which everyone was selfish. You would try to protect your own interests, although you would get little help from anyone else. (This is Hobbes's "state of nature.")
- You would be worst off in a situation in which you were benevolent while others were selfish. Other people could stab you in the back when it was to their advantage, but you would never do the same. You would come out on the short end every time. (This is the "sucker's payoff.")

Now this is exactly the kind of array that gives rise to the Prisoner's Dilemma. Based on these assessments, you should adopt the selfish strategy:

(1) Either other people will respect your interests or they won't.

(2) If they do respect your interests, you will be better off not respecting theirs, at least whenever that would be to your advantage. This will be the optimum situation—you get to be a free rider.

(3) If they do not respect your interests, then it will be foolish for you to respect theirs. That will land you in the worst possible situation—you get the sucker's payoff.

(4) Therefore, regardless of what other people do, you are better off adopting the policy of looking out for yourself. You should be selfish.

And now we come to the catch: Other people, of course, can reason in the same way, and the result will be that we end up in Hobbes's state of nature. Everyone will be selfish, willing to knife anyone who gets in their way. In that situation, each of us would be worse off than if we all cooperated.

To escape the dilemma, we need another enforceable agreement, this time to obey the rules of mutually respectful social living. As before, cooperation will not yield the optimum outcome (which we would get if we were selfish while others were benevolent), but it will lead to a better result than if we independently pursued our own interests. We need, in David Gauthier's words, to "bargain our way into morality." We can do that if we can establish sanctions to ensure that, if we respect other people's interests, they will respect ours.

6.3. Some Advantages of the Social Contract Theory

Morality, on this theory, consists in the rules that rational people will accept, on the condition that others accept them as well. The strength of this theory is due, in large measure, to the fact that it provides plausible answers to some difficult questions.

1. *What moral rules are we bound to follow, and how are those rules justified?* The morally binding rules are the ones that facilitate harmonious social living. We could not live together in peace if we allowed murder, assault, theft, lying, promise breaking, and so on. The rules forbidding those acts are therefore justified by their tendency to promote harmony and cooperation. On the other hand, "moral rules" that condemn prostitution, sodomy, and sexual promiscuity cannot be justified on these grounds. How is social living hampered by private, voluntary sexual activity? How would it benefit us to agree to such rules? What people do behind closed doors is outside the scope of the social contract. Such rules, therefore, have no claim on us.

2. *Why is it rational for us to follow the moral rules?* We *agree to* follow the moral rules because we benefit from living in a place where the rules are accepted. However, we *actually do* follow the rules—we keep our end of the bargain—because the rules will be enforced, and it is rational for us to avoid punishment. Why don't you kidnap your boss? Because you might get caught.

But what if you think you won't get caught? Why follow the rules then? To answer this question, first note that you don't want *other* people to break the rules when they think they can avoid punishment—you don't want other people to commit murder, assault, and so on, just because they think they can get away with it. After all, they might be murdering or assaulting *you*. For this reason, we want others to accept the contract in more than a frivolous or lighthearted way. We want them to form a *firm intention* to hold up their end of the bargain; we want them to become the sort of people who won't be tempted to stray. And, of course, they will demand the same of us, as part of the agreement. But once we have this firm intention, it is rational to act on it. Why don't you kidnap your boss, when you think you can get away with it? Because you've made a firm decision not to be that sort of person.

3. *Under what circumstances is it rational to break the rules?* We agree to obey the rules on the condition that others obey them as well. But when someone else breaks the rules, he releases us from our obligations toward him. For example, suppose someone refuses to help you in circumstances in which he clearly should. If later on he needs your help, you may rightly feel that you have no duty to help him.

The same point explains why it is permissible to punish those who have broken the law. Lawbreakers are treated differently from normal citizens—in punishing them, we treat them in ways that are not normally permitted. Why is such treatment justified? First, it is justified because the criminal has violated the condition of reciprocity: The rules of social living limit what *we* can do only if others accept the same restrictions on what *they* can do. Therefore, by violating the rules, criminals release us from our obligations toward them and leave themselves open to retaliation. Second, the purpose of the state is to enforce the rules of social living. If we are to live together without fear, it cannot be left up to the individual whether he or she will attack others, steal from them, and so on. Attaching sanctions to these rules is the only way to enforce them. It follows that the state needs to punish.

4. *How much can morality demand of us?* Morality seems to require that we be impartial, that is, that we give no greater weight to our own interests than to the interests of others. But suppose you face a situation in which you must choose between your own death and the deaths of five other people. Impartiality, it seems, would require you to choose your own death; after all, there are five of them and only one of you. Are you morally bound to sacrifice yourself?

Philosophers have often felt uneasy about this sort of example; they have felt instinctively that somehow there are limits to what morality can demand of us. Therefore, they have traditionally said that such heroic actions are *supererogatory*— that is, above and beyond the call of duty, admirable when they occur but not morally required. Yet it is hard to explain why such actions are not required. If morality demands impartial behavior, and it is better that one person die rather than five, then you should be required to sacrifice yourself.

What does the Social Contract Theory say about this? Suppose the question is whether to have the rule "If you can save many lives by sacrificing your own life, then you must do so." Would it be rational to accept this rule, on the condition that everyone else accepts it? Presumably, it would be. After all, each of us is more likely to benefit from this rule than to be harmed by it—you're more likely to be among those saved than to be the one and only person who gives up her life. Thus, it may seem that the Social Contract Theory does require moral heroism.

But this is not so. On the Social Contract Theory, morality consists in the rules that rational people will accept *on the condition that others accept them as well.* However, it would not be rational to make an agreement that we don't expect others to follow. Can we expect other people to follow this rule of self-sacrifice—can we expect strangers to give up their lives for us? We cannot. Most people won't be that benevolent, even if they have promised to be. Can we expect the threat of punishment to *make them* that benevolent? Again, we cannot; people's fear of death is likely to overwhelm any fear they have of punishment. Thus, there is a natural limit to the amount of self-sacrifice that the social contract can require: Rational people will not agree to rules so demanding that others won't follow them. In this way, the Social Contract Theory explains a feature of morality that other theories can't explain.

6.4. The Problem of Civil Disobedience

Moral theories should help us understand particular moral issues. The Social Contract Theory is based on ideas about how to set up society, so it is especially good at dealing with questions about social institutions. Our obligation to obey the law arises from the social contract. But are we ever justified in defying the law? And if so, when?

The great modern examples of civil disobedience are taken from the Indian independence movement led by Mohandas K. Gandhi (1869–1948) and the American civil rights movement led by Martin Luther King, Jr. (1929–1968). Both movements were characterized by public, conscientious, nonviolent refusal to comply with the law. In 1930, Gandhi and his followers marched to the coastal village of Dandi, where they defied British law by distilling salt from saltwater. The British had been controlling salt production so they could force the Indian peasants to buy it at high prices. In America, Dr. King led the Montgomery Bus Boycott, which began after Rosa Parks was arrested on December 1, 1955, for refusing to give up her bus seat to a white man. Parks was defying one of the "Jim Crow" laws designed to enforce racial segregation in the South. Gandhi and King, the two greatest proponents of nonviolence in the 20th century, were both murdered by assassins.

Their movements had importantly different goals. Gandhi and his followers did not recognize the right of the British to govern India; they wanted to replace British rule with an entirely different system. King and his followers, however, did not question the legitimacy of the American government. They objected only to particular laws and social policies that they regarded as unjust—so unjust, in fact, that they felt released from any obligation to obey them.

In his "Letter from the Birmingham City Jail" (1963), King describes the frustration and anger that arise

> when you have seen vicious mobs lynch your mothers and fathers at will and drown your sisters and brothers at whim; when you have seen hate-filled policemen curse, kick, brutalize and even kill your black brothers and sisters with impunity; when you see the vast majority of your twenty million Negro brothers smothering in an airtight cage of poverty in the midst of an affluent society; when you

> suddenly find your tongue twisted and your speech stam-
> mering as you seek to explain to your six-year-old daughter
> why she can't go to the public amusement park that has
> just been advertised on television, and see tears welling up
> in her little eyes when she is told that Funtown is closed to
> colored children, and see the depressing clouds of inferi-
> ority begin to form in her little mental sky. . . .

The problem was not only that racial segregation, with all its
attendant evils, was enforced by social custom; it was a matter of
law as well, law that black citizens were denied a voice in formu-
lating. When urged to rely on ordinary democratic processes,
King pointed out that all attempts to use these processes had
failed. And as for "democracy," he said, that word had no meaning to Southern blacks: "Throughout the state of Alabama all
types of conniving methods are used to prevent Negroes from
becoming registered voters and there are some counties without a single Negro registered to vote despite the fact that the
Negro constitutes a majority of the population." King believed,
therefore, that blacks had no choice but to defy the unjust laws
and to accept the consequences by going to jail.

Today we remember King as a great moral leader. At the
time, however, his strategy of civil disobedience was highly controversial. Many liberals expressed sympathy for his goals but
didn't agree with his tactic of breaking the law. An article published in the *New York State Bar Journal* in 1965 expressed the typical worries. After assuring his readers that "long before Dr. King
was born, I espoused, and still espouse, the cause of civil rights
for all people," Louis Waldman, a prominent New York lawyer,
argues:

> Those who assert rights under the Constitution and the
> laws made thereunder must abide by that Constitution
> and the law, if that Constitution is to survive. They cannot
> pick and choose; they cannot say they will abide by those
> laws which they think are just and refuse to abide by those
> laws which they think are unjust. . . .
>   The country, therefore, cannot accept Dr. King's
> doctrine that he and his followers will pick and choose,
> knowing that it is illegal to do so. I say, such doctrine is
> not only illegal and for that reason alone should be aban-
> doned, but that it is also immoral, destructive of the prin-
> ciples of democratic government, and a danger to the very
> civil rights Dr. King seeks to promote.

Waldman had a point: If the legal system is basically decent, then defying the law is on its face a bad thing, because such defiance weakens respect for the law generally. To meet this objection, those who advocated civil disobedience needed to show why defiance of the law was justified. One argument, which King often used, was that the evils being opposed were so serious, so numerous, and so difficult to fight that civil disobedience was justified as a last resort. The end justifies the means, though the means are regrettable. This argument may be enough to answer Waldman's objections. But there is a more profound reply available, suggested by the Social Contract Theory.

Why do we have an obligation to obey the law in the first place? According to the Social Contract Theory, it is because each of us participates in a complicated arrangement whereby we gain certain benefits in return for accepting certain burdens. The benefits are the benefits of social living: We escape the state of nature and live in a society in which we are secure and enjoy basic rights. To gain these benefits, we agree to uphold the institutions that make them possible. This means that we must obey the law, pay our taxes, and so forth—these are the burdens we accept in return.

But what if things are arranged so that some people in society are not granted the rights enjoyed by others? What if, instead of protecting them, "hate-filled policemen curse, kick, brutalize and even kill [them] with impunity?" What if some citizens are "smothering in an airtight cage of poverty" while being denied the opportunity to acquire a decent education? Under such circumstances, the social contract is not being honored. By asking the disadvantaged group to obey the law and respect society's institutions, we are asking them to accept the burdens of social living while being denied its benefits.

This line of reasoning suggests that civil disobedience is not an undesirable "last resort" for socially disenfranchised groups. Rather, it is the most natural and reasonable means of expressing protest. For when the disadvantaged are denied the benefits of social living, they are released from the contract that would otherwise require them to follow society's rules. This is the deepest argument for civil disobedience, and the Social Contract Theory presents it clearly and forcefully.

6.5. Difficulties for the Theory

The Social Contract Theory is one of the major options in current moral philosophy, along with Utilitarianism, Kantianism, and Virtue Ethics. It is easy to see why; the theory seems to explain a great deal about moral life. Two important objections, however, have been made against it.

First, it is said that the Social Contract Theory is based on a historical fiction. We are asked to imagine that people once lived in isolation from one another, that they found this intolerable, and that they eventually banded together, agreeing to follow social rules of mutual benefit. But none of this ever happened. It is just a fantasy. So of what relevance is it? To be sure, if people *had* come together in this way, we could explain their obligations to one another as the theory suggests: They would be obligated to obey the rules because they had agreed to do so. But even then, there would be problems. Was the agreement unanimous? If not, what of the people who did not sign up—are they *not* required to act morally? And if the contract was made a long time ago, are we bound by the agreements of our ancestors? But anyway, there never was such a contract, and so nothing can be explained by appealing to it. As one critic wisecracked, the social contract "isn't worth the paper it's not written on."

To be sure, none of us ever signed a "real" contract— there is no piece of paper bearing our signatures. However, the contract theorist might say, a social arrangement like the one described does exist: There is a set of rules that everyone recognizes as binding on them, and we all benefit from the fact that these rules are generally followed. Each of us accepts the benefits conferred by this arrangement; and, more than that, we expect and encourage other people to observe the rules. This is a description of the actual state of affairs; it is not fictitious. And, by accepting the benefits of this arrangement, we incur an obligation to do our part—in other words, to follow the rules. We are thus bound by an *implicit* social contract. It is "implicit" because we become a party to it not through our words but through our actions, as we accept the benefits of social living.

Thus, the story of the "social contract" need not be intended as a description of historical events. Rather, it is a useful analytical tool, based on the idea that we may understand our moral obligations *as if* they had arisen in this way. Consider the following situation: Suppose you come upon a group of people playing an elaborate game. It looks like fun, and you join in. After a while, however, you begin to break some of the rules, because that looks like more fun. When the other players protest, you say that you never promised to follow the rules. However, this is irrelevant. Perhaps nobody promised to obey; but, by joining the game, each person implicitly agreed to abide by the rules that make the game possible. It is *as though* they had all agreed. Morality is like this. The "game" is social living; we derive enormous benefits from it; but, to get those benefits, we have to play by the rules.

That response to the first objection, however, is ineffective. When a game is in progress, and you join in, it is obvious that you *choose* to join in, since you could have just walked away. For that reason, you must respect the rules of the game, or you will rightly be regarded as a nuisance. By contrast, someone born into today's big cooperative world does not *choose* to be part of it—rather, one is thrust into it, and the exit costs are severe. How could you opt out? You might become a survivalist and never use electricity, roads, the water service, and so on. But that would be a great burden. By not taking that option, must you be acquiescing to society's rules? Alternatively, you might leave the country. But what if you don't like the social rules that exist in any of the other countries, either? Moreover, as David Hume (1711–1776) observed, many people are not "free to leave their country" in any meaningful sense:

> Can we seriously say that a poor peasant . . . has a free choice to leave his country, when he knows no foreign language or manners, and lives from day to day by the small wages which he acquires? We may as well assert that a man, by remaining [on a ship], freely consents to the dominion of the master, though he was carried on board while asleep, and must leap into the ocean and perish the moment he leaves. . . .

Does the first objection therefore refute the Social Contract Theory? I don't think so. The contract theorist may say this: Participating in a sensible social scheme is rational; it really is in one's best interest. *This is why the rules are valid*—because they benefit those who live under them. If someone doesn't agree to the rules, the rules still apply to him; he's just being irrational. Suppose, for example, that a survivalist forgoes the benefits of social living. May he then refuse to pay his taxes? He may not, because even he would be better off paying his taxes *and* enjoying the benefits of clean water, paved roads, indoor plumbing, and so on. The survivalist might not want to play the game, but the rules still apply to him, because it would really and truly be in his interest to join in.

This defense of the Social Contract Theory abandons the idea that morality is based on an agreement. However, it holds fast to the idea that morality consists in rules of mutual benefit. It also accords with the definition of the theory we gave earlier: *Morality consists in the set of rules, governing behavior, that rational people will accept, on the condition that others accept them as well.* Rational people will agree to the mutually beneficial rules.

The second objection is more troubling. Some individuals cannot benefit us. Thus, according to the Social Contract Theory, we can ignore their interests; they have no claim on us. This implication is unacceptable.

There would be at least four vulnerable groups:

- Human infants
- Nonhuman animals
- Future generations
- Oppressed populations

Suppose, for example, that a sadist wanted to torment a cat or a small child. *He* would not benefit from a system of rules forbidding the torture of infants and animals; after all, the infant and the cat cannot benefit him, and he wants to practice his cruel behavior. Of course, the infant's parents, and the cat's owners, would be indirectly harmed under such a system, and they might want to retaliate against the sadist. In such a situation, it is hard to know what moral rules would be valid. But suppose the sadist found some abandoned children or some stray cats out in the woods. Now the Social Contract Theory cannot condemn him even if he commits acts of the greatest cruelty.

Or consider future generations. They cannot benefit us. We'll be dead before they are even born. But we can profit at their expense. Why shouldn't we pollute the lakes and coat the skies in carbon dioxide? Why shouldn't we bury toxic waste in containers that will fall apart in a hundred years? It would not be against *our* interests to allow such actions; it would only harm our descendants. So, we may do so. Or consider oppressed populations. When the Europeans colonized new lands, why weren't they morally allowed to enslave the native inhabitants? After all, the native inhabitants did not have the weapons to put up a good fight. The Europeans could benefit most by enslaving them, not by cooperating with them.

This objection does not concern some minor aspect of the theory; it goes right to the root of the tree. The Social Contract Theory is grounded in self-interest and reciprocity; thus, it seems unable to recognize the moral duties we have to individuals who cannot benefit us.

CHAPTER 7

The Utilitarian Approach

> Given our present perspective, it is amazing that Christian
> ethics down through the centuries could have accepted almost
> unanimously the . . . doctrine that "the end does not justify the
> means." We have to ask now, "If the end does not justify the means,
> what does?" The answer is, obviously, "Nothing!"
>
> JOSEPH FLETCHER, *MORAL RESPONSIBILITY* (1967)

7.1. The Revolution in Ethics

The late 18th and 19th centuries witnessed an astonishing series of upheavals: The modern nation-state emerged from the French Revolution and the wreckage of the Napoleonic empire; the revolutions of 1848 showed the transforming power of the ideas of "liberty, equality, and fraternity"; and in America, a country with a new kind of constitution was created, and its bloody civil war would put an end to slavery in Western civilization. All the while, the Industrial Revolution was bringing about a complete restructuring of society.

It is not surprising that new ideas about ethics emerged during this era. Jeremy Bentham (1748–1832) made a powerful argument for a novel conception of morality. Morality, he urged, is not about pleasing God, nor is it about being faithful to abstract rules. Morality is about making the world as happy as possible. Bentham believed in one ultimate moral principle, namely, the Principle of Utility. This principle requires us, in all circumstances, to produce the most happiness that we can.

Bentham was the leader of a group of philosophical radicals whose aim was to reform the laws and institutions of England along utilitarian lines. One of his followers was James Mill, the distinguished Scottish philosopher, historian, and economist. James Mill's son, John Stuart Mill (1806–1873), would become the leading advocate of utilitarian moral theory. John Stuart's advocacy was even more elegant and persuasive than Bentham's. Mill's little book, *Utilitarianism* (1861), is still required reading for serious students of ethics.

At first glance, the Principle of Utility may not seem like such a radical idea; in fact, it may seem too obvious to mention. Who could argue with the idea that we should oppose suffering and promote happiness? Yet, in their own way, Bentham and Mill were as revolutionary as the other two great intellectual innovators of the 19th century, Darwin and Marx.

To understand why the Principle of Utility was so radical, we have to appreciate what it *leaves out* of its picture of morality: Gone are all references to God or to abstract moral rules "written in the heavens." Morality is no longer to be understood as faithfulness to some divinely given code or some set of inflexible rules. As Peter Singer (1946–) would later put it, morality is not "a system of nasty puritanical prohibitions . . . designed to stop people [from] having fun." Rather, the point of morality is the happiness of beings in this world, and nothing more; and we are permitted—even required—to do whatever is necessary to promote that happiness. This was a revolutionary idea.

The utilitarians were, as I said, social reformers as well as philosophers. They intended their doctrine to make a difference, not only in thought but in practice. To illustrate this, we will briefly examine the implications of their ideas for three practical issues: euthanasia, marijuana, and the treatment of nonhuman animals. These issues do not by any means exhaust the practical applications of Utilitarianism; nor are they necessarily the ones that utilitarians would find most pressing. But they do give us a good sense of how utilitarians approach moral issues.

7.2. First Example: Euthanasia

Sigmund Freud (1856–1939), the legendary psychologist, was diagnosed with oral cancer after a lifetime of cigar smoking. During his final years, Freud's health went up and down, but in January of 1939 a large swelling appeared in the back of his mouth, and he would have no more good days. Freud's cancer was active and inoperable, and he was also suffering from heart failure. As his bones decayed, they cast off a foul smell, driving away his favorite dog. Mosquito netting had to be draped over his bed to keep flies away.

On September 21, at the age of 83, Freud took his friend and personal physician, Max Schur, by the hand and said, "My dear Schur, you certainly remember our first talk. You promised me then not to forsake me when my time comes. Now it's nothing but torture and makes no sense any more." Forty years earlier Freud had written, "What has the individual come to . . . if one no longer dares to disclose that it is this or that man's turn to die?" Dr. Schur said he understood Freud's request. He injected Freud with a drug in order to end his life. "He soon felt relief," Dr. Schur wrote, "and fell into a peaceful sleep."

Did Max Schur do anything wrong? On the one hand, he was motivated by noble sentiments—he loved his friend and wanted to relieve his misery. Moreover, Freud had asked to die. All this argues for a lenient judgment. On the other hand, according to the dominant moral tradition in our culture, what Schur did was unacceptable.

The dominant moral tradition in our culture is Christianity. Christianity holds that human life is a gift from God, and only God may decide when it will end. The early church prohibited all killing, believing that Jesus's teachings permitted no exceptions to the rule. Later, some exceptions were made, chiefly to allow capital punishment and killing in war. But other kinds of killing, including suicide and euthanasia, remained forbidden. To summarize the church's doctrine, theologians formulated the rule: *the intentional killing of innocent people is always wrong.* This conception, more than anything else, has shaped Western attitudes about the morality of killing. That is why we may be reluctant to excuse Max Schur, even if he acted from noble motives. He intentionally killed an innocent person; therefore, according to our moral tradition, what he did was wrong.

Utilitarianism takes a very different approach. It asks, which action available to Max Schur would have produced the greatest balance of happiness over unhappiness? The person with the most at stake in the situation was Sigmund Freud. If Schur had not killed him, Freud would have lived on, in wretched pain. How much unhappiness would this have involved? It is hard to say precisely; but Freud's condition was so bad that he preferred death. Killing him ended his agony. Therefore, utilitarians have concluded that euthanasia, in such a case, is morally right.

Although this kind of argument is very different from what one finds in the Christian tradition, the classical utilitarians did not think they were advocating an atheistic or anti-religious philosophy. Bentham suggests that the faithful would endorse, not condemn, the utilitarian standpoint if only they viewed God as a *benevolent* creator. He writes:

> The dictates of religion would coincide, in all cases, with those of utility, were the Being, who is the object of religion, universally supposed to be as benevolent as he is supposed to be wise and powerful. . . . But among the [advocates] of religion . . . there seem to be but few (I will not say how few) who are real believers in his benevolence. They call him benevolent in words, but they do not mean that he is so in reality.

The morality of mercy killing might be a case in point. How, Bentham might ask, could a benevolent God forbid the killing of Sigmund Freud? If someone were to say that God is kind but he requires Freud to suffer more before dying, this would be exactly what Bentham means by "calling him benevolent in words, but not meaning that he is so in reality."

The majority of religious people disagree with Bentham, and not only our moral tradition but our legal tradition has evolved under the influence of Christianity. Among Western nations, euthanasia is legal in only a handful of countries. In the United States, it is simply murder, and a doctor who intentionally kills her patient could spend the rest of her life in prison. What would Utilitarianism say about this? If, on the utilitarian view, euthanasia is moral, should it also be legal?

In general, we don't want to outlaw morally acceptable behavior. Bentham was trained in the law, and he thought of the Principle of Utility as a guide for both legislators and ordinary people. The purpose of the law, he thought, is to promote the welfare of all citizens. In order to serve this purpose, it should restrict people's freedom as little as possible. In particular, no activity should be outlawed unless that activity is harmful or dangerous to others. Bentham opposed, for example, laws regulating the sexual conduct of consenting adults. But it was

Mill who gave this principle its most eloquent expression, in his book *On Liberty* (1859):

> the only purpose for which power can be rightfully exercised over any member of a civilized community, against his will, is to prevent harm to others. His own good, either physical or moral, is not a sufficient warrant. . . . Over himself, over his own body and mind, the individual is sovereign.

Thus, for the classical utilitarians, laws against euthanasia are not only contrary to the general welfare, they are also unjustified restrictions on people's ability to control their own lives. When Max Schur killed Sigmund Freud, he was helping Freud end his life in the manner that Freud had chosen. No harm was caused to anyone else, and so it was no one else's business. Consistent with his utilitarian philosophy, Bentham is said to have requested euthanasia in his final days, although we do not know whether this request was granted.

7.3. Second Example: Marijuana

William Bennett was America's first "drug czar." From 1989 to 1991, as President George H. W. Bush's top advisor on drug policy, he advocated the aggressive enforcement of U.S. drug laws. Bennett, who holds a Ph.D. in philosophy, said, "The simple fact is that drug use is wrong. And the moral argument, in the end, is the most compelling argument." Bennett's "moral argument," it seems, is just the assertion that drug use is wrong, by its very nature. What would utilitarians think about this? For them, there is no "simple fact" as to whether drug use is immoral. Rather, the moral argument must address the complex question of whether drug use increases or decreases happiness. Let's think about one drug in particular: marijuana. What would a utilitarian say about the ethics of pot?

People have strong feelings on this topic. Younger people who use drugs might be defensive and deny that pot causes any harm at all; older people who don't use drugs might be judgmental and fail to distinguish marijuana from harder drugs like cocaine and methamphetamine. A good utilitarian will try to put such feelings aside. What are the pros and cons of marijuana, according to Utilitarianism?

The main benefit of pot is the pleasure it brings. Marijuana can greatly enhance the pleasure of sensory activities, such as eating, listening to music, and having sex. This fact is almost never mentioned in public discussion; people seem to assume that enjoyment is irrelevant to morality. Utilitarians, however, disagree. For them, the whole issue is whether pot increases or decreases happiness.

How pleasurable is marijuana? Some people love it; some people don't like it; and a lot depends on whether it is used in a comfortable setting. Thus, it is hard to generalize. But the facts suggest that many people enjoy getting high. Marijuana is the most popular illicit drug in America: One-third of Americans have tried it; 6% have used it in the past month; and Americans spend more than $10 billion per year on it, despite the threat of prison.

What unhappiness does marijuana cause? Some of the charges made against it are unfounded. First, marijuana does not cause violence; pot tends to make people passive, not aggressive. Second, marijuana is not a "gateway drug" that causes people to crave and use harder drugs. Often, people do use pot before using harder drugs, but that is because pot is so widely available. In neighborhoods where crack cocaine is easier to get, people usually try crack first. Third, marijuana is not highly addictive. According to the experts, it is less addictive than caffeine. Utilitarians do not want to base their assessment on false information.

Marijuana, however, does have some real disadvantages, which the utilitarian must weigh against the benefits. First, some people do get addicted to pot. For the addict, quitting is painful and difficult. Second, long-term heavy use can cause mild cognitive damage, which may decrease happiness. Third, getting high all the time would make a person unproductive. Fourth, *smoking* pot is bad for your respiratory system; one joint may be as bad for your lungs as about six cigarettes. However, ingesting marijuana in other ways—for example, by baking it into brownies—should not be bad for your lungs at all.

What do utilitarians conclude from all this? When we look at the harms and benefits, the occasional use of pot hardly seems to be a moral issue at all; there are no known disadvantages to it. Thus, utilitarians consider casual use to be a matter of personal preference. Heavy marijuana use raises more complex issues. Does the pleasure one gets from long-term, heavy use outweigh the disadvantages? It is not easy to say, and utilitarians may disagree on this issue.

So far we've been discussing the individual's decision of whether to use marijuana. What about the law—should pot be illegal, according to Utilitarianism? Utilitarians believe that people tend to be happier if they have more freedom, and drug laws do reduce freedom. This counts in favor of legalization. What other factors are relevant?

If marijuana were legal, more people would use it, and several worries arise from that fact: society as a whole might become less productive; taxpayers might get stuck with the medical bills of heavy users; and more people might drive while high. It should be noted, however, that marijuana impairs driving ability only slightly, because people who are stoned drive cautiously and defensively.

On the other hand, society would be better off insofar as marijuana replaced alcohol as a drug of abuse: stoned citizens are unproductive, but alcoholics miss even more work because alcohol creates a hangover; alcoholism is especially expensive in terms of health care; alcohol impairs driving ability much more than pot does; and, finally, drunks are far more violent than potheads. One possible benefit of legalizing pot would be fewer alcoholics.

Also, there are two big costs to maintaining the current laws. The first is the lost revenue for society. With marijuana illegal, society spends money on criminal enforcement; with marijuana legal, society collects money from taxing pot. Legalizing marijuana in the U.S. would save about $7.7 billion per year in enforcement costs, and it would generate between $2.4 and $6.2 billion in tax revenue, depending on whether pot was taxed normally or at the higher rate at which alcohol and tobacco are now taxed.

But the greatest cost is the harm done to the offenders. In the U.S., over 850,000 marijuana arrests are made each year, and more than 44,000 people are currently in prison for marijuana offenses. Not only is being arrested and incarcerated horrible, but ex-cons have trouble finding decent jobs. Utilitarians care about these harms, even though the harms are inflicted on lawbreakers who knew they might be punished.

Thus, almost all utilitarians favor the legalization of marijuana. On the whole, marijuana is less harmful than alcohol or cigarettes, which Western societies already tolerate. However, utilitarians must be flexible; if new evidence emerges, showing marijuana to be more harmful than was previously thought, then the utilitarian view might change.

7.4. Third Example: Nonhuman Animals

The treatment of nonhumans has traditionally been regarded as a trivial matter. Christians believe that man alone is made in God's image and that animals do not have souls. Thus, by the natural order of things, we can treat animals in any way we like. Saint Thomas Aquinas (1225–1274) summed up the traditional view when he wrote:

> Hereby is refuted the error of those who said it is sinful for a man to kill brute animals; for by the divine providence they are intended for man's use in the natural order. Hence it is not wrong for man to make use of them, either by killing them or in any other way whatever.

But isn't it wrong to be *cruel* to animals? Aquinas concedes that it is, but he says the reason has to do with human welfare, not the welfare of the animals:

> And if any passages of Holy Scripture seem to forbid us to be cruel to brute animals, for instance to kill a bird with its young, this is either to remove man's thoughts from being cruel to other men, lest through being cruel to animals one becomes cruel to human beings; or because injury to an animal leads to the temporal hurt of man, either of the doer of the deed, or of another. . . .

Thus, people and animals are in separate moral categories. Animals have no moral standing of their own; we are free to treat them in any way we please.

Spelled out as baldly as this, the traditional doctrine might make us a little nervous: It seems extreme in its lack of concern for nonhuman animals, many of which are, after all, intelligent and sensitive creatures. Yet only a little reflection is needed to see how much of our conduct is actually guided by this doctrine. We eat animals; we use them as experimental subjects in our laboratories; we use their skins for clothing and their heads as wall ornaments; we make them the objects of our amusement in zoos and rodeos; and we track them down and kill them for sport.

If one is uncomfortable with the theological "justification" of these practices, Western philosophers have offered plenty of secular ones. Philosophers have said that animals are not *rational*, that they lack the ability to *speak*, or that they are simply not *human*—and all these are given as reasons why their interests are outside the sphere of moral concern.

The utilitarians, however, would have none of this. On their view, what matters is not whether an animal has a soul, is rational, or any of the rest. All that matters is whether it can experience happiness and unhappiness. If an animal can suffer, then we have a duty to take that into account when deciding what to do. In fact, Bentham argues that whether an animal is human or nonhuman is just as irrelevant as whether she is black or white. He writes:

> The day *may* come when the rest of the animal creation may acquire those rights which never could have been withholden from them but by the hand of tyranny. The French have already discovered that the blackness of the skin is no reason why a human being should be abandoned without redress to the caprice of a tormentor. It may one day come to be recognized that the number of the legs, the villosity of the skin, or the termination of the *os sacrum* are reasons equally insufficient for abandoning a sensitive being to the same fate. What else is it that should trace the insuperable line? Is it the faculty of reason, or perhaps the faculty of discourse? But a full-grown horse or dog is beyond comparison a more rational, as well as a more conversable animal, than an infant of a day or a week or even a month old. But suppose they were otherwise, what would it avail? The question is not, Can they *reason*? nor Can they *talk*? but, Can they *suffer*?

If a human is tormented, why is it wrong? Because that person suffers. Similarly, if a nonhuman is tormented, it also suffers. Whether it is a *human* or an *animal* that suffers is simply irrelevant. To Bentham and Mill, this line of reasoning was conclusive. Humans and nonhumans are equally entitled to moral concern.

This view may seem as extreme, in the opposite direction, as the traditional view that grants animals no moral standing at all. Are animals really to be regarded as the equals of humans? In some ways, Bentham and Mill thought so, but they did not believe that animals and humans must always be treated in the same way. There are factual differences between them that will often justify differences in treatment. For example, because of their intellectual capacities, humans can take pleasure in things that nonhumans cannot enjoy—mathematics, literature, strategy games, and so on. And, similarly, humans' superior capacities make them capable of frustrations and disappointments that other animals cannot experience. Thus, our duty to promote happiness entails a duty to promote those special enjoyments for humans, as well as to prevent any special harms they might suffer. At the same time, however, we have a moral duty to take into account the suffering of animals, and their suffering counts equally with any similar suffering experienced by a human.

In 1970, the British psychologist Richard D. Ryder coined the term "speciesism" to refer to the idea that animal interests matter less than human interests. Utilitarians believe that speciesism is discrimination against other species, just as racism is discrimination against other races. Ryder wonders how we can possibly justify experiments such as these:

- In Maryland in 1996, scientists used beagle dogs to study septic shock. They cut holes in the dogs' throats and placed *E. coli*-infected clots into their stomachs. Within three weeks, most of the dogs had died.
- In Taiwan in 1997, scientists dropped weights onto rats' spines in order to study spinal injury. The researchers found that greater injuries were caused by dropping the weights from greater heights.
- Since the 1990s, chimpanzees, monkeys, dogs, cats, and rodents have been used to study alcoholism. After addicting the animals to alcohol, scientists have observed such symptoms as vomiting, tremor, anxiety, and seizures. When the animals are in alcoholic withdrawal, scientists have induced convulsions by lifting them by their tails, by giving them electric shocks, and by injecting chemicals into their brains.

The utilitarian argument is simple enough. We should judge actions right or wrong depending on whether they cause more happiness or unhappiness. The animals in these experiments were obviously caused terrible suffering. Was there any compensating gain in happiness that justified it? Was greater unhappiness being prevented, for other animals or for humans? If not, the experiments were morally unacceptable.

This style of argument does not imply that all animal experiments are immoral. Rather, it suggests judging each one on its own merits. The utilitarian principle does, however, imply that experiments which cause a lot of pain require significant justification. We cannot simply assume that, in dealing with nonhumans, anything goes.

But criticizing animal experiments is too easy for most of us. We may feel self-righteous or superior because we do not do such research ourselves. All of us, however, are involved in cruelty when we eat meat. The facts about meat production are more disturbing than any facts about animal experimentation.

Most people believe, in a vague way, that slaughterhouses are unpleasant, but that animals raised for food are otherwise treated humanely. In fact, farm animals live in abhorrent conditions before being taken off to slaughter. Veal calves, for example, spend twenty-four hours per day in pens so small that they cannot turn around, lie down comfortably, or even twist their heads around to get rid of parasites. The producers put them in tiny pens to save money and to keep their meat tender. The cows clearly miss their mothers, and like human infants, they want something to suck, so they try in vain to suck the sides of their wooden stalls. The calves are also fed a diet deficient in iron and roughage, in order to keep their meat pale and tasty. Their craving for iron becomes so strong that they will lick at their own urine, if they're allowed to turn around—which normally they would never do. Without roughage, the calves cannot form a cud to chew. For this reason, they cannot be given straw bedding, since they would eat it, in an attempt to consume roughage. So, for these animals, the slaughterhouse is not an unpleasant end to an otherwise contented existence.

Among farm animals, veal calves suffer the most. Chickens, turkeys, pigs, and adult cows, however, all live in horrible conditions before being slaughtered. The utilitarian argument on these matters is simple enough. The system of meat production causes enormous suffering for the animals with no compensating benefits. Therefore, we should abandon that system. We should either become vegetarians or else treat our animals humanely before killing them.

What is most revolutionary in all this is simply the idea that the interests of nonhuman animals *count*. We normally assume, as the dominant tradition of our society teaches, that human beings alone are worthy of moral consideration. Utilitarianism challenges that basic assumption and insists that the moral community must be expanded to include all creatures whose interests are affected by what we do. Human beings are in many ways special, and an adequate morality must acknowledge that. But we are not the only animals on this planet, and an adequate morality must acknowledge that fact as well.

CHAPTER 8

The Debate over Utilitarianism

The utilitarian doctrine is that happiness is desirable, and the only thing desirable, as an end; all other things being desirable as means to that end.

JOHN STUART MILL, *UTILITARIANISM* (1861)

Man does not strive after happiness; only the Englishman does that.

FRIEDRICH NIETZSCHE, *TWILIGHT OF THE IDOLS* (1889)

8.1. The Classical Version of the Theory

Classical Utilitarianism, the theory of Bentham and Mill, can be summarized in three propositions: (a) Actions are to be judged right or wrong solely by virtue of their consequences; nothing else matters. (b) In assessing consequences, the only thing that matters is the amount of happiness or unhappiness that is created; everything else is irrelevant. (c) Each person's happiness counts the same. Thus, right actions are those that produce the greatest balance of happiness over unhappiness, with each person's happiness counted as equally important.

This theory has profoundly influenced both ethicists and social scientists. Most ethicists, however, reject Utilitarianism, due to a slew of objections. In what follows, we will examine some of these objections and consider whether they succeed. In doing so, we will grapple with some fundamental questions in moral philosophy.

8.2. Is Pleasure All That Matters?

The question *What things are good?* is different from the question *What actions are right?* and Utilitarianism answers the second question by reference to the first. Right actions are the ones that produce the most good. But what is good? The utilitarian reply is: happiness. As Mill puts it, "The utilitarian doctrine is that happiness is desirable, and the only thing desirable, as an end; all other things being desirable as means to that end."

But what is happiness? According to the classical utilitarians, happiness is pleasure. Utilitarians understand "pleasure" broadly, to include all mental states that feel good. A sense of accomplishment, a delicious taste, and the heightened awareness that comes at the climax of a suspenseful movie are all examples of pleasure. The idea that pleasure is the one ultimate good—and pain the one ultimate evil—has been known since antiquity as Hedonism. Hedonism has always been attractive because of its simplicity and because it expresses the plausible notion that things are good or bad because of how they make us *feel.* Yet a little reflection seems to reveal flaws in this theory.

Consider these two examples:

- *You think someone is your friend, but he ridicules you behind your back.* No one tells you, so you never know. Is this unfortunate for you? Hedonists would have to say it is not, because you are never caused any pain. Yet we feel there is something bad going on. You are "being made a fool of," even though you are unaware of it and you suffer no unhappiness.
- *A promising young pianist's hands are injured in a car accident so that she can no longer play.* Why is this bad for her? Hedonists would say it is bad because it causes her pain and eliminates a source of joy for her. But suppose she finds something else that she enjoys just as much— suppose, for example, that she gets as much pleasure from watching hockey on TV as she once got from playing the piano. Why is her accident now a tragedy? The hedonist can only say that she will feel frustrated and upset whenever she thinks of what might have been, and her misfortune is that she feels bad. But this explanation gets things backwards. It is not as though, by feeling upset, she has turned a neutral situation into a bad one. On the contrary, the bad situation is what made her unhappy. She could have had a career as a concert pianist, and now she cannot. That is the tragedy. We cannot eliminate the tragedy just by getting her to cheer up and watch hockey.

Both of these examples make the same basic point: We value all sorts of things, such as artistic creativity and friendship, for their own sakes. It makes us happy to have them, but that's not the only reason we value them. It seems like a misfortune to lose them, even if there is no loss of happiness.

For this reason, there are not many hedonists among contemporary philosophers. Those sympathetic to Utilitarianism have therefore sought a way to formulate their view without assuming a hedonistic account of the good. Some, such as the English philosopher G. E. Moore (1873–1958), have tried to compile short lists of things to be regarded as valuable in themselves. Moore suggested that there are three obvious intrinsic goods—pleasure, friendship, and aesthetic enjoyment—and so right actions are those actions that increase the world's supply of these things. Other utilitarians bypass the question of how many things are good in themselves, saying only that right actions are the ones that have the best results, however that is measured. Still others say that we should act so as to maximize the satisfaction of people's *preferences.* I won't discuss the merits and demerits of these varieties of Utilitarianism. I mention them only to note that, although Hedonism has largely been rejected, contemporary utilitarians have not found it difficult to carry on.

8.3. Are Consequences All That Matter?

To determine whether an action is right, utilitarians believe that we should look at *what will happen as a result of doing it.* This idea is essential to the theory. If things other than consequences are important in determining what is right, then Utilitarianism is incorrect. Here are three arguments that attack the theory at just this point.

Justice. In 1965, writing in the racially charged climate of the American Civil Rights movement, H. J. McCloskey asks us to consider the following case:

> Suppose a utilitarian were visiting an area in which there was racial strife, and that, during his visit, a Negro rapes a white woman, and that race riots occur as a result of the crime. . . . Suppose too that our utilitarian is in the area of the crime when it is committed such that his

testimony would bring about the conviction of [whomever he accuses]. If he knows that a quick arrest will stop the riots and lynchings, surely, as a utilitarian, he must conclude that he has a duty to bear false witness in order to bring about the punishment of an innocent person.

Such an accusation would have bad consequences—the innocent man would be convicted—but there would be enough good consequences to outweigh them: The riots and lynchings would be stopped. The best outcome would be achieved by lying; therefore, according to Utilitarianism, lying is the thing to do. But, the argument continues, it would be wrong to bring about the conviction of an innocent person. Therefore, Utilitarianism, which implies otherwise, must be incorrect.

According to the critics of Utilitarianism, this argument illustrates one of the theory's most serious shortcomings, namely, that it is incompatible with the ideal of justice. Justice requires that we treat people fairly, according to the merits of their particular situations. In McCloskey's example, Utilitarianism requires that we treat someone unfairly. Thus, Utilitarianism cannot be right.

Rights. Here is an example from the U.S. Court of Appeals. In the case of *York v. Story* (1963), arising out of California:

> In October, 1958, appellant [Ms. Angelynn York] went to the police department of Chino for the purpose of filing charges in connection with an assault upon her. Appellee Ron Story, an officer of that police department, then acting under color of his authority as such, advised appellant that it was necessary to take photographs of her. Story then took appellant to a room in the police station, locked the door, and directed her to undress, which she did. Story then directed appellant to assume various indecent positions, and photographed her in those positions. These photographs were not made for any lawful or legitimate purpose.
>
> Appellant objected to undressing. She stated to Story that there was no need to take photographs of her in the nude, or in the positions she was directed to take, because the bruises would not show in any photograph. . . .
>
> Later that month, Story advised appellant that the pictures did not come out and that he had destroyed them.

Instead, Story circulated these photographs among the personnel of the Chino police department. In April, 1960, two other officers of that police department, appellee Louis Moreno and defendant Henry Grote, acting under color of their authority as such, and using police photographic equipment located at the police station, made additional prints of the photographs taken by Story. Moreno and Grote then circulated these prints among the personnel of the Chino police department.

Ms. York brought suit against these officers and won. Her legal rights had clearly been violated. But what of the *morality* of the officers' behavior? Utilitarianism says that actions are defensible if they produce a favorable balance of happiness over unhappiness. This suggests that we compare the amount of unhappiness caused to York with the amount of pleasure the photographs gave to Officer Story and the others. It is at least possible that more happiness than unhappiness was created. In that case, the utilitarian conclusion would be that their actions were morally acceptable. But this seems to be a perverse way of thinking. Why should the pleasure of Story and his friends matter at all? They had no right to treat York in this way, and the fact that they enjoyed doing so hardly seems a relevant defense.

Consider a related case. Suppose a Peeping Tom spied on a woman through her bedroom window and secretly took pictures of her undressed. Further suppose that he did this without being detected and that he used the photographs entirely for his own pleasure, without showing them to anyone. Now, under these circumstances, the only consequence of his action seems to be an increase in his own happiness. No one else, including the woman, is caused any unhappiness at all. How, then, could Utilitarianism deny that the Peeping Tom's actions are right? But it is evident to moral common sense that they are not right. Thus, Utilitarianism appears to be unacceptable.

The key point to be drawn from this argument is that Utilitarianism is at odds with the idea that people have *rights* that may not be trampled on merely because one anticipates good results. In these cases, the woman's right to privacy is violated. But it would not be difficult to think of similar cases in which other rights are at issue—the right to worship freely, the right to speak your mind, or even the right to live. It may happen that good purposes are served, from time to time, by violating these rights. But we do not think that our rights should be set aside so easily. The notion of a personal right is not a utilitarian notion. Quite the opposite: It is a notion that places limits on how an individual may be treated, regardless of the good purposes that might be accomplished.

Backward-Looking Reasons. Suppose you have promised someone you will do something—say, you promised to meet her at the mall this afternoon. But when the time comes to go, you don't want to do it; you need to catch up on some work and you would rather stay home. You try to call her up to cancel, but she isn't answering her cell phone. What should you do? Suppose you judge that the utility of getting your work done slightly outweighs the irritation your friend will experience from being stood up. Appealing to the utilitarian standard, you might conclude that staying home is better than keeping your promise. However, this does not seem correct. The fact that you *promised* imposes an obligation on you that you cannot escape so easily. Of course, if a great deal were at stake—if, for example, you had to rush your mother to the hospital—you would be justified in breaking the promise. But a *small* gain in utility cannot overcome the obligation created by your promise; the obligation should mean something, morally. Thus, Utilitarianism once again seems mistaken.

This criticism is possible because Utilitarianism cares only about the *consequences* of our actions. However, we normally think that considerations about the past are important, too. You made a promise to your friend, and that's a fact about the past. Utilitarianism seems faulty because it excludes such backward-looking reasons.

Once we understand this point, we can think of other examples of backward-looking reasons. The fact that someone committed a crime is a reason to punish him. The fact that someone did you a favor last week may be a reason why you should do her a favor next week. The fact that you did something to hurt someone may be a reason to make it up to him now. These are all facts about the past that are relevant to determining our obligations. But Utilitarianism makes the past irrelevant, and so it seems flawed.

8.4. Should We Be Equally Concerned for Everyone?

The last part of Utilitarianism says that we must treat each person's happiness as equally important—or as Mill put it, we must be "as strictly impartial as a disinterested and benevolent spectator." Stated abstractly, this sounds plausible, but it has troublesome implications. One problem is that the requirement of "equal concern" places too great a demand on us; another problem is that it disrupts our personal relationships.

The Charge That Utilitarianism Is Too Demanding. Suppose you are on your way to the movies when someone points out that the money you are about to spend could be used to provide food for starving people or inoculations for third-world children. Surely, those people need food and medicine more than you need to see Brad Pitt and Angelina Jolie. So you forgo your entertainment and donate the money to a charitable agency. But that is not the end of it. By the same reasoning, you cannot buy new clothes, a car, a digital camera, or a PlayStation. Probably you should move into a cheaper apartment. After all, what's more important—that you have these luxuries, or that children have food?

In fact, faithful adherence to the utilitarian standard would require you to give away your resources until you've lowered your standard of living to the level of the neediest people you could help. Or rather, you'd need to leave yourself just enough to maintain your job, so that you can keep on giving. Although we admire people who do this, we do not regard them as simply doing their duty. Instead, we regard them as saintly people whose generosity goes *beyond* the call of duty. Philosophers call such actions *supererogatory*. But Utilitarianism seems unable to recognize this moral category.

The problem is not merely that Utilitarianism would require us to give up most of our material resources. It would also prevent us from carrying on our individual lives. We all have goals and projects that make our lives meaningful. An ethic that requires the subordination of everything to the promotion of the general welfare would force us to abandon those endeavors. Suppose you are a web designer, not getting rich but making a decent living; you have two children whom you love; and on weekends, you like to perform with an amateur theater group. In addition, you enjoy reading history. How could there be anything wrong with this? But judged by the utilitarian standard, you are leading a morally unacceptable life. After all, you could be doing a lot more good if you spent your time in other ways.

The Charge That Utilitarianism Disrupts Our Personal Relationships. In practice, none of us is willing to treat everyone equally, since that would require us to abandon our special relationships with friends and family. We are all deeply partial where our family and friends are concerned. We love them, and we go to great lengths to help them. To us, they are not just members of the great crowd of humanity—they are special. But all this is inconsistent with impartiality. When you are impartial, you miss out on intimacy, love, affection, and friendship.

At this point, Utilitarianism seems to have lost touch with reality. What would it be like to be no more concerned for one's husband or wife than for strangers whom one has never met? The very idea is absurd; not only is it profoundly contrary to normal human emotions, but loving relationships could not even exist apart from special responsibilities and obligations. Again, what would it be like to treat one's children with no greater love than one has for strangers? As John Cottingham puts it, "A parent who leaves his child to burn" because "the building contains someone else whose future contribution to the general welfare promises to be greater, is not a hero; he is (rightly) an object of moral contempt, a moral leper."

8.5. The Defense of Utilitarianism

These arguments add up to an overwhelming indictment of Utilitarianism. The theory, which at first seemed so plausible and progressive, now seems indefensible. It seems at odds with justice and individual rights, and it seems unable to account for the place of backward-looking reasons in justifying conduct. It would have us give away most of our possessions and spoil the personal relationships that mean everything to us.

Not surprisingly, the combined weight of these arguments has prompted most philosophers to abandon the theory altogether. Some philosophers, however, continue to believe in Utilitarianism. Three general defenses have been offered.

The First Defense: Denying That the Consequences Would Be Good. The first defense says that the anti-utilitarian arguments make unrealistic assumptions. Most of those arguments share a common strategy. The critic describes a case and then says that Utilitarianism requires a certain action—bearing false witness, violating someone's rights, and so on. But, the critic says, these actions are obviously immoral. Therefore, Utilitarianism is incorrect.

But this strategy succeeds only if we agree that the actions described really would have the best consequences. And why should we agree with that? In the real world, lying under oath does *not* have good consequences. Suppose, in the case described by McCloskey, the "utilitarian" tried to incriminate the innocent man in order to stop the riots. He probably would not succeed; his lie might be found out, and then the situation would be even worse than before. Even if the lie succeeded, the real culprit would remain at large and might commit more crimes. Also, if the guilty party were caught later on, which is always possible, the liar would be in deep trouble, and confidence in the criminal justice system would erode. The moral is that although one might *think* that one can bring about the best consequences by such behavior, one cannot be certain of it. In fact, experience teaches the opposite: Utility is not served by framing innocent people.

The same goes for the other cases cited in the anti-utilitarian arguments. Lying, violating people's rights, breaking one's promises, and severing one's personal relationships all have bad consequences. Only in philosophers' imaginations is it otherwise. In the real world, Peeping Toms are caught, just as Officer Story and his cohorts were caught, and their victims suffer. In the real world, when people lie, their reputations suffer and other people get hurt; and when people break their promises and fail to return favors, they lose their friends.

So that is the first defense. How effective is it? Unfortunately, it contains more bluster than substance. While it is true that *most* acts of false witness and the like have bad consequences, it cannot be said that *all* such acts have bad consequences. At least once in a while, one can bring about a good result by doing something repugnant to moral common sense. Therefore, in at least some real-life cases, Utilitarianism will conflict with common sense. Moreover, even if the anti-utilitarian arguments had to rely exclusively on fictitious examples, those arguments would nevertheless retain their power, for showing that Utilitarianism has unacceptable consequences in hypothetical cases is a valid way of critiquing it. The first defense, then, is weak.

The Second Defense: The Principle of Utility Is a Guide for Choosing Rules, Not Acts. Revising a theory is a two-step process: first, you identify which feature of the theory needs work; second, you change only that feature, leaving the rest of the theory intact. What feature of Classical Utilitarianism is causing the trouble?

The troublesome assumption is that *each individual action* should be evaluated by reference to the Principle of Utility. If on a certain occasion you are tempted to lie, classical Utilitarianism says that whether it would be wrong depends on the consequences of *telling that particular lie;* whether you should keep a particular promise depends on the consequences of *keeping that particular promise;* and so on for each of the examples we have considered. If what we care about is the consequences of particular actions, then we can always dream up circumstances in which a horrific action will have the best consequences.

Therefore, the new version of Utilitarianism modifies the theory so that individual actions are no longer judged by the Principle of Utility. Instead, we first ask what *set of rules* is optimal, from a utilitarian viewpoint. In other words, what rules should we follow to maximize happiness? Individual acts are then judged right or wrong according to whether they are acceptable or unacceptable by these rules. This new version of the theory is called "Rule-Utilitarianism," to distinguish it from the original theory, now commonly called "Act-Utilitarianism."

Rule-Utilitarianism has an easy answer to the anti-utilitarian arguments. An act-utilitarian would incriminate the innocent man in McCloskey's example because the consequences of *that particular act* would be good. But the rule-utilitarian would not reason in that way. She would first ask, What rules of conduct tend to promote the most happiness? One good rule is "Don't bear false witness against the innocent." That rule is simple, easy to remember, and following it will almost always increase happiness. By appealing to it, the rule-utilitarian can conclude that in McCloskey's example we should not testify against the innocent man.

Analogous reasoning can be used to establish rules against violating people's rights, breaking promises, lying, betraying one's friends, and so on. We should accept such rules because following them, as a regular practice, promotes the general happiness. We no longer judge acts by their utility but by their conformity with these rules. Thus, Rule-Utilitarianism cannot be convicted of violating our moral common sense. In shifting emphasis from the justification of acts to the justification of rules, Utilitarianism has been brought into line with our intuitive judgments.

However, a serious problem with Rule-Utilitarianism arises when we ask whether the ideal rules have *exceptions*. Must the rules be followed no matter what? What if a "forbidden" act would greatly increase the overall good? The rule-utilitarian might give any one of three replies.

First, if she says that in such cases we may violate the rules, it looks like she wants to assess actions on a case-by-case basis. This is Act-Utilitarianism, not Rule-Utilitarianism.

Second, she might suggest that we formulate the rules so that violating them never will increase happiness. For example, instead of using the rule "Don't bear false witness against the innocent," we might use the rule "Don't bear false witness against the innocent, unless doing so would achieve some great good." If we change all of the rules in this way, then Rule-Utilitarianism will be exactly like Act-Utilitarianism in practice; the rules we follow will always tell us to choose the act that promotes the most happiness in our particular circumstances. But now Rule-Utilitarianism does not provide a response to the anti-utilitarian arguments; like Act-Utilitarianism, it tells us to incriminate the innocent, to break our promises, to spy on people in their homes, and so on.

Finally, the rule-utilitarian might stand her ground and say that we should never break the rules, even to promote happiness. J. J. C. Smart (1920–) says that such a person suffers from an irrational "rule worship." Whatever one thinks of that, this version of Rule-Utilitarianism is not really a utilitarian theory. Utilitarians care solely about happiness and about consequences; but this theory, in addition, cares about following rules. The theory is thus a mix of Utilitarianism and something else entirely. To paraphrase one writer, this type of Rule-Utilitarianism is like a rubber duck: just as a rubber duck is not a kind of duck, this type of Rule-Utilitarianism is not a kind of Utilitarianism. And so, we cannot defend Utilitarianism by appealing to it.

The Third Defense: "Common Sense" Is Wrong. Finally, some utilitarians have offered a very different response to the objections. Upon being told that Utilitarianism conflicts with common sense, they respond, "So what?" Looking back at his own defense of Utilitarianism, J. J. C. Smart writes:

> Admittedly utilitarianism does have consequences which are incompatible with the common moral consciousness, but I tended to take the view "so much the worse for the common moral consciousness." That is, I was inclined to reject the common methodology of testing general ethical principles by seeing how they square with our feelings in particular instances.

This breed of utilitarian—hard-nosed and unapologetic—can offer three responses to the anti-utilitarian arguments.

The First Response: All Values Have a Utilitarian Basis. Critics of Utilitarianism say that the theory can't make sense of some of our most important values—such as the value we attach to truth telling, promise keeping, respecting others' privacy, and loving our children. Consider, for example, lying. The main reason not to lie, the critics say, has nothing to do with bad consequences. The reason is that lying is dishonest; it betrays people's trust. That fact has nothing to do with the utilitarian calculation of benefits. Honesty has a value over and above any value that the utilitarian can acknowledge. The same is true of promise keeping, respecting others' privacy, and loving our children.

But according to philosophers such as Smart, we should think about these values one at a time and consider why they're important. When people lie, the lies are often discovered, and those betrayed feel hurt and angry. When people break their promises, they irritate their neighbors and alienate their friends. Someone whose privacy is violated may feel humiliated and want to withdraw from others. When people don't care more about their own children than they do about strangers, their children feel unloved, and one day they too may become unloving parents. All these things reduce happiness. Far from being at odds with the idea that we should be honest, dependable, respectful, and loving to our children, Utilitarianism explains why those things are good.

Moreover, apart from the utilitarian explanation, these duties would seem inexplicable. What could be stranger than the idea that lying is wrong "in itself," apart from any harm it causes? And how could people have a "right to privacy" unless respecting that right brought about some benefit? On this way of thinking, Utilitarianism is not incompatible with common sense; on the contrary, Utilitarianism justifies the common-sense values we have.

The Second Response: Our Gut Reactions Can't Be Trusted When Cases Are Exceptional. Although some cases of injustice serve the common good, those cases are exceptions. Lying, promise breaking, and violations of privacy usually lead to unhappiness, not happiness. This observation forms the basis of another utilitarian response.

Consider again McCloskey's example of the person tempted to bear false witness. Why do we immediately and instinctively believe it to be wrong to bear false witness against an innocent person? The reason, some say, is that throughout our lives we have seen lies lead to misery and misfortune. Thus, *we instinctively condemn all lies, even ones that do not lead to misery and misfortune.* But when we condemn lies that are beneficial, our intuitive faculties are misfiring. Experience has taught us to condemn lies because they reduce happiness. Now, however, we are condemning lies that increase happiness. When confronting unusual cases, such as McCloskey's, perhaps we should trust the Principle of Utility more than our gut instincts.

The Third Response: We Should Focus on *All* the Consequences. When we're asked to consider a "despicable" action that maximizes happiness, the action is often presented in a way that encourages us to focus on its bad effects, and not on its good effects. If instead we focus on *all* the effects of the act, Utilitarianism seems more plausible.

Consider yet again the McCloskey example. McCloskey says it would be wrong to convict an innocent man because that would be unjust. But what about the *other* innocent people who will be hurt if the rioting and lynchings continue? What about the pain that will be endured by those who are beaten and tormented by the mob? What about the deaths that will occur if the man doesn't lie? Children will lose their parents, and parents will lose their children. Of course, we never want to face a situation like this. But if we must choose between securing the conviction of one innocent person and allowing the deaths of several innocent people, is it so unreasonable to think that the first option is preferable?

And consider again the objection that Utilitarianism is too demanding because it tells us to use our resources to feed starving children rather than using those resources to eat at restaurants. If we focus our thoughts on those who would starve, do the demands of Utilitarianism seem so unreasonable? Isn't it self-serving of us to say that Utilitarianism is "too demanding," rather than saying that we should feed starving children?

This strategy works better for some cases than for others. Consider the Peeping Tom. The unapologetic utilitarian will tell us to consider the pleasure *he* gets from spying on unsuspecting women. If he gets away with it, what harm has been done? Why should his action be condemned? Most people will condemn his behavior, despite the utilitarian arguments. Utilitarianism, as Smart suggests, cannot be fully reconciled with common sense.

Nevertheless, some philosophers think that Act-Utilitarianism is a perfectly defensible doctrine that does not need to be modified. Even so, it must be said that Utilitarianism is a radical doctrine that challenges many commonsense assumptions. In this respect, it does what good philosophy always does—it makes us think about things that we take for granted.

8.6. Concluding Thoughts

If we consult what Smart calls our "common moral consciousness," many considerations other than utility seem morally important. But Smart is right to warn us that "common sense" cannot be trusted. That may turn out to be Utilitarianism's greatest contribution. The deficiencies of moral common sense become obvious if we think for only a moment. Many white people once felt that there was an important difference between whites and blacks, so that the interests of whites were somehow more important. Trusting the "common sense" of their day, they might have insisted that an adequate moral theory should accommodate this "fact." Today, no one worth listening to would say such a thing, but who knows how many other irrational prejudices are still part of our moral common sense? At the end of his classic study of race relations, *An American Dilemma,* Nobel Laureate Gunnar Myrdal (1898–1987) reminds us:

> There must be still other countless errors of the same sort that no living man can yet detect, because of the fog within which our type of Western culture envelops us. Cultural influences have set up the assumptions about the mind, the body, and the universe with which we begin; pose the questions we ask; influence the facts we seek; determine the interpretation we give these facts; and direct our reaction to these interpretations and conclusions.

Could it be, for example, that future generations will look back in disgust at the way affluent people in the 21st century enjoyed their comfortable lives while third-world children died of easily preventable diseases? Or at the way we confined and slaughtered helpless animals? If so, they might note that utilitarian philosophers were ahead of their time in condemning such things.

CHAPTER 9

A *re There Absolute Moral Rules?*

You may not do evil that good may come.
SAINT PAUL, *LETTER TO THE ROMANS* (ca. 50 A.D.)

9.1. Harry Truman and Elizabeth Anscombe

Harry S. Truman will always be remembered as the man who made the decision to drop the atomic bombs on Hiroshima and Nagasaki. When he became president in 1945, following the death of Franklin D. Roosevelt, Truman knew nothing about the bomb; Roosevelt's advisors had to fill him in. The Allies were winning the war in the Pacific, they said, but at a terrible cost. Plans had been drawn up for an invasion of Japan, but that battle would be even bloodier than the D-Day assault on Normandy had been. Using the atomic bomb on one or two Japanese cities might bring the war to a speedy end, making the invasion unnecessary.

Truman was at first reluctant to use the new weapon. The problem was that each bomb would obliterate an entire city—not just the military targets, but the hospitals, schools, and homes. Women, children, old people, and other noncombatants would be wiped out along with the military personnel. The Allies had bombed cities before, but Truman sensed that the new weapon made the issue of noncombatants even more acute. Moreover, the United States was on record as condemning attacks on civilian targets. In 1939, before America had entered the war, President Roosevelt had sent a message to the governments of France, Germany, Italy, Poland, and Great Britain, denouncing the bombardment of cities in the strongest terms. He had called it an "inhuman barbarism":

> The ruthless bombing from the air of civilians . . . which has resulted in the maiming and in the death of thousands of defenseless men, women, and children, has sickened the hearts of every civilized man and woman, and has profoundly shocked the conscience of humanity. If resort is had to this form of inhuman barbarism during the period of the tragic conflagration with which the world is now confronted, hundreds of thousands of innocent human beings who have no responsibility for, and who are not even remotely participating in, the hostilities which have now broken out, will lose their lives.

Truman expressed similar thoughts when he decided to authorize the bombings. He wrote in his diary that "I have told the Sec. of War, Mr. Stimson, to use it so that military objectives and soldiers and sailors are the target and not women and children. . . . He and I are in accord. The target will be a purely military one." It is hard to know what to make of this, since Truman knew that the bombs would destroy whole cities. Nonetheless, it is clear that he was worried about the issue of noncombatants.

It is also clear that Truman was sure of his decision. Winston Churchill, the wartime leader of Great Britain, met with Truman shortly before the bombs were dropped, and he later wrote, "the decision whether or not to use the atomic bomb to compel the surrender of Japan was never even an issue. There was unanimous, automatic, unquestioned agreement around our table. . . ." After signing the final order, thus sealing the fate of Hiroshima, Truman later said that he "slept like a baby."

Elizabeth Anscombe, who died in 2001, was a 20-year-old student at Oxford University when World War II began. At that time, she co-authored a controversial pamphlet arguing that Britain should not go to war because countries at war inevitably end up fighting by unjust means. "Miss Anscombe," as she was always known—despite her 59-year marriage and her seven children—would go on to become one of the 20th century's most distinguished philosophers, and the greatest woman philosopher in history.

Miss Anscombe was also a Catholic, and her religion was central to her life. Her ethical views reflected traditional Catholic teachings. In 1968, she celebrated Pope Paul VI's affirmation of the church's ban on contraception and wrote a pamphlet explaining why artificial birth control is immoral. Late in her life, she was arrested while protesting outside a British abortion clinic. She also accepted the church's teaching about the ethical conduct of war, which brought her into conflict with Truman.

Harry Truman and Elizabeth Anscombe crossed paths in 1956. Oxford University was planning to give Truman an honorary degree in thanks for America's wartime help, and those proposing the honor thought it would be uncontroversial. But Anscombe and two other faculty members opposed the idea. Although they lost, they forced a vote on what would otherwise have been a rubber-stamp approval. Then, while the degree was being conferred, Anscombe knelt outside the hall, praying.

Anscombe wrote another pamphlet, this time explaining that Truman was a murderer because he had ordered the bombings of Hiroshima and Nagasaki. Of course, Truman thought the bombings were justified—they had shortened the war and saved lives. For Anscombe, this was not good enough. "For men to choose to kill the innocent as a means to their ends," she wrote, "is always murder." To the argument that the bombings saved more lives than they took, she replied, "Come now: if you had to choose between boiling one baby and letting some frightful disaster befall a thousand people—or a million people, if a thousand is not enough—what would you do?"

Anscombe's example was apt. The bomb blast at Hiroshima, which ignited birds in midair, did lead to babies being boiled: People died in rivers, reservoirs, and cisterns, trying in vain to escape the heat. Anscombe's point was that *some things may not be done, no matter what*. It does not matter if we could accomplish some great good by boiling a baby; it is simply wrong. Anscombe believed in a host of such rules. Under no circumstances, she said, may we intentionally kill innocent people; worship idols; make a false profession of faith; engage in sodomy or adultery; punish one person for the acts of another; or commit treachery, which she describes as "obtaining a man's confidence in a grave matter by promises of trustworthy friendship and then betraying him to his enemies."

Of course, many philosophers do not agree; they insist that any rule may be broken if the circumstances demand it. Anscombe says of them:

> [N]one of these philosophers displays any consciousness that there is such an ethic, which he is contradicting: it is pretty well taken for obvious among them all that a prohibition such as that on murder does not operate in the face of some consequences. But of course the strictness of the prohibition has as its point that *you are not to be tempted by fear or hope of consequences.*

Anscombe's husband, Peter Geach (1916–), agreed with this. Anscombe and Geach were the 20th century's foremost philosophical champions of the doctrine that moral rules are absolute.

9.2. The Categorical Imperative

The idea that moral rules have no exceptions is hard to defend. It is easy enough to explain why we *should* break a rule—we can simply point to cases in which following the rule would have terrible consequences. But how can we defend *not* breaking the rule in such cases? It is a daunting assignment. We might say that moral rules are God's inviolable commands. Apart from that, what can be said?

Before the 20th century, there was one major philosopher who believed that moral rules are absolute. Immanuel Kant (1724–1804) argued that lying is wrong under any circumstances. He did not appeal to theological considerations; he held, instead, that reason always forbids lying. To see how he reached this conclusion, we will begin by looking at his general theory of ethics.

Kant observed that the word *ought* is often used nonmorally:

- If you want to become a better chess player, you *ought* to study the games of Garry Kasparov.
- If you want to go to college, you *ought* to take the SAT.

Much of our conduct is governed by such "oughts." The pattern is this: We have a certain desire (to become a better chess player, to go to college); we recognize that a certain course of action will help us get what we want (studying Kasparov's games, taking the SAT); and so we follow the indicated plan.

Kant called these "hypothetical imperatives" because they tell us what to do *provided that* we have the relevant desires. A person who did not want to improve her chess would have no reason to study Kasparov's games; someone who did not want to go to college would have no reason to take the SAT. Because the binding force of the "ought" depends on having the relevant desire, we can escape its force by letting go of the desire. Thus, I can avoid taking the SAT by deciding that I don't want to go to college.

Moral obligations, by contrast, do not depend on having particular desires. The form of a moral obligation is not "*If* you want so-and-so, then you ought to do such-and-such." Instead, moral requirements are *categorical:* They have the form "You ought to do such-and-such, *period.*" The moral rule is not, for example, that you ought to help people *if* you care about them or *if* you want to be a good person. Instead, the rule is that you should help people *no matter what* your desires are. That is why moral requirements cannot be escaped simply by saying "But I don't care about that."

Hypothetical "oughts" are easy to understand. They merely require us to do what is necessary to achieve our goals. Categorical "oughts," on the other hand, are mysterious. How can we be obligated to behave in a certain way regardless of our goals? Kant has an answer. Just as hypothetical "oughts" are possible because we have *desires,* categorical "oughts" are possible because we have *reason.* Categorical oughts, Kant says, are derived from a principle that every rational person must accept: the Categorical Imperative. In his *Foundations of the Metaphysics of Morals* (1785), he expresses the Categorical Imperative as follows:

> Act only according to that maxim by which you can at the same time will that it should become a universal law.

This principle provides a way to tell whether an act is morally permissible. When you are thinking about doing something, ask what rule you would be following if you actually did it. This rule will be the "maxim" of your act. Then ask whether you would be willing for your maxim to become a universal law. In other words, would you allow your rule to be followed by all people at all times? If so, then your maxim is sound, and your act is acceptable. But if not, then your act is forbidden.

Kant gives several examples to explain how this works. Suppose, he says, a man needs money, but no one will lend it to him unless he promises to pay it back—which he knows he won't be able to do. Should he make a false promise to get the loan? If he did, his maxim would be: *Whenever you need a loan, promise to repay it, even if you know you can't.* Now, could he will that this rule become a universal law? Obviously not, because it would be self-defeating. Once this rule became a universal practice, no one would believe such promises, and so no one would make loans based on them.

Kant gives another example, about giving aid. Suppose, he says, I refuse to help others in need, saying to myself, "What do I care? Let each person fend for himself." This, again, is a rule that I cannot will to be a universal law. For at some time in the future, I myself will need the help of others, and I will not want them to turn away.

9.3. Kant's Arguments on Lying

Being a moral agent, then, means guiding one's conduct by "universal laws"—moral rules that hold, without exception, in all circumstances. Kant believed that there are many such rules. However, it will be useful for us to focus on the rule against lying. Kant had especially strong feelings on the topic. He said that lying under any circumstances is "the obliteration of one's dignity as a human being."

Kant offered two arguments for an absolute rule against lying.

1. His main argument relies on the Categorical Imperative. We could not will a universal law that allows us to lie, Kant said, because such a law would be self-defeating. As soon as lying became common, people would stop believing each other. Lying would then have no point, and in a sense it would become impossible, because nobody would pay attention to what you say. Therefore, Kant reasoned, lying cannot be allowed. And so, it is forbidden under any circumstances.

This argument has a flaw, which will become clearer with an example. Suppose it was necessary to lie to save someone's life. Should you do it? Kant would have us reason as follows:

(1) We should do only those actions that conform to rules that we could will to be adopted universally.

(2) If you were to lie, you would be following the rule "It is okay to lie."

(3) This rule could not be adopted universally, because it would be self-defeating: People would stop believing one another, and then it would do no good to lie.

(4) Therefore, you should not lie.

Although Anscombe agreed with Kant's conclusion, she was quick to point out an error in his reasoning. The difficulty arises in step (2). Why should we say that, if you lied, you would be following the rule, "It is okay to lie?" Perhaps your maxim would be: "I will lie when doing so would save someone's life." *That* rule would not be self-defeating. It could become a universal law. And so, by Kant's own theory, it would be all right for you to lie. The Categorical Imperative is useless, Anscombe says, without some guidance as to how to formulate rules.

2. Many of Kant's contemporaries thought that his insistence on absolute rules was strange, and they said so. One reviewer challenged him with this example: Imagine that someone is fleeing from a murderer and tells you that he is going home to hide. Then the murderer comes by and asks you where the man is. You believe that, if you tell the truth, you will be aiding in a murder. Furthermore, the killer is already headed the right way, so if you simply remain silent, the worst result is likely. What should you do? Let's call this the Case of the Inquiring Murderer. Under these circumstances, most of us think you should lie. After all, which is more important: telling the truth or saving someone's life?

Kant responded in an essay with the charmingly old-fashioned title "On a Supposed Right to Lie from Altruistic Motives," in which he gives a second argument against lying. Perhaps, he says, the man on the run has actually left his home, and by telling the truth you would lead the killer to look in the wrong place. However, if you lie, the murderer may wander away and discover the man leaving the area, in which case you would be responsible for his death. Whoever lies, Kant says, "must answer for the consequences, however unforeseeable they were, and pay the penalty for them. . . ." Kant states his conclusion in the tone of a stern schoolmaster: "To be truthful . . . in all deliberations, therefore, is a sacred and absolutely commanding decree of reason, limited by no expediency."

This argument may be stated in a general form: We are tempted to make exceptions to the rule against lying because in some cases we think the consequences of truthfulness will be bad and the consequences of lying will be good. However, we can never be certain about what the consequences will be—we cannot *know* that good results will follow. The results of lying might be unexpectedly bad. Therefore, the best policy is to avoid the known evil—lying—and let the consequences come as they may. Even if the consequences are bad, they will not be our fault, for we will have done our duty.

A similar argument, we may note, would apply to Truman's decision to drop the atomic bombs on Hiroshima and Nagasaki. The bombs were dropped in the hope that the war could be swiftly concluded. But Truman did not know for sure that this would happen. The Japanese might have hunkered down, and the invasion might still have been necessary. So, Truman was betting hundreds of thousands of lives on the mere hope that good results might ensue.

The problems with this argument are obvious enough—so obvious, in fact, that it is surprising that a philosopher of Kant's caliber was not more sensitive to them. In the first place, the argument depends on an unreasonably pessimistic view of what we can know. Sometimes we can be quite confident of what the consequences of our actions will be, in which case we need not hesitate because of uncertainty. Moreover—and this is more significant, philosophically—Kant seems to assume that although we would be morally responsible for any bad consequences of lying, we would not be responsible for any bad consequences of telling the truth. Suppose, as a result of our telling the truth, the murderer found his victim and killed him. Kant seems to assume that we would be blameless. But can we escape responsibility so easily? After all, we aided the murderer. This argument, then, is not convincing.

Thus, Kant has failed to prove that lying is always wrong. The Case of the Inquiring Murderer shows what a tough row he chose to hoe. While Kant believes that any lie "obliterates one's dignity as a human being," common sense says that some lies are harmless. In fact, we have a name for them: white lies. Aren't white lies acceptable—or even required—when they can be used to save someone's life? This points to the main difficulty for the belief in absolute rules: shouldn't a rule be broken when following it would be disastrous?

9.4. Conflicts between Rules

Suppose it is held to be absolutely wrong to do X in any circumstances and also wrong to do Y in any circumstances. Then what about the case in which a person must choose between doing X and doing Y? This kind of conflict seems to show that moral rules can't be absolute.

Is there any way that this objection can be met? One way is to deny that such conflicts ever actually occur. Peter Geach took just this view, appealing to God's providence. We can describe fictitious cases in which there is no way to avoid violating one of the absolute rules, he said, but God will not permit such circumstances to exist in the real world. Geach asks:

> "But suppose circumstances are such that observance of one Divine law, say the law against lying, involves breach of some other absolute Divine prohibition?"—If God is rational, he does not command the impossible; if God governs all events by his providence, he can see to it that circumstances in which a man is inculpably faced by a choice between forbidden acts do not occur. Of course such circumstances . . . are consistently describable; but God's providence could ensure that they do not in fact arise. Contrary to what nonbelievers often say, belief in the existence of God does make a difference to what one expects to happen.

Do such cases actually occur? There is no doubt that serious moral rules sometimes clash. During World War II, Dutch fishermen smuggled Jewish refugees to England in their boats, and sometimes they would be stopped by Nazi patrols. The Nazi captain would call out and ask the Dutch captain where he was going, who was on board, and so forth. The fishermen would lie and be allowed to pass. Clearly, the fishermen had only two options: either they lie, or they let everyone on their boat be killed. No third alternative was available; they could not, for example, remain silent or outrun the Nazis. Thus, Geach appears to have been naïve. Terrible dilemmas do occur in the real world.

If such dilemmas occur, then doesn't this disprove the existence of absolute moral rules? Suppose, for example, the two rules "It is wrong to lie" and "It is wrong to facilitate the murder of innocent people" are both taken to be absolute. The Dutch fishermen would have to do one of these things; therefore, a moral view that absolutely prohibits both is incoherent.

This type of argument is impressive, but it is also limited. It can be levied only against *pairs* of absolute moral rules; two rules are needed to create the conflict. The argument won't stop someone from believing that there is just one absolute rule. And, in a way, everyone does. "Do what is right" is a moral principle we all believe in, which admits of no exceptions. We should always do what is right. However, this rule is so formal that it is trivial—we believe it because it doesn't really say anything. That rule is not the kind of absolute moral rule that Kant, Geach, and Anscombe wanted to argue for.

9.5. Kant's Insight

The philosopher Alasdair MacIntyre (1929–) remarks, "For many who have never heard of philosophy, let alone of Kant, morality is roughly what Kant said it was"—that is, a system of rules that one must follow from a sense of duty. Yet few contemporary philosophers would defend Kant's Categorical Imperative. As we have seen, that principle is beset by serious, perhaps insurmountable, problems. Nonetheless, it might be a mistake to give up on Kant's conception too quickly. Is there some basic idea underlying the Categorical Imperative that we might accept, even if we reject Kant's way of expressing it? I believe that there is.

Remember that Kant viewed the Categorical Imperative as binding on rational agents simply because they are rational; in other words, a person who did not accept this principle would be guilty not merely of being immoral but of being irrational. This is a compelling idea. But what exactly does this mean? In what sense would it be irrational to reject the Categorical Imperative?

Note that a moral judgment must be backed by good reasons—if it is true that you ought (or ought not) to do such-and-such, then there must be a reason why you should (or should not) do it. For example, you may think that you ought not to set forest fires because property would be destroyed and people would be killed. The Kantian twist is to point out that *if you accept any considerations as reasons in one case, you must also accept them as reasons in other cases.* If there is another case in which property would be destroyed and people killed, you must accept this as a reason for action in that case, too. It is no good saying that you can accept reasons some of the time, but not all the time; or that other people must respect them, but not you. Moral reasons, if they are valid at all, are binding on all people at all times. This is a requirement of consistency, and Kant was right to think that no rational person may deny it.

This insight has some important implications. It implies that a person cannot regard herself as special, from a moral point of view: She cannot consistently think that she is permitted to act in ways that are forbidden to others, or that her interests are more important than other people's interests. As one commentator remarked, I cannot say that it is all right for me to drink your beer and then complain when you drink mine. Moreover, it implies that there are rational constraints on what we may do: We may want to do something—say, to drink someone else's beer—but recognize that we cannot consistently do it because we cannot at the same time accept the implication that he may drink our beer. If Kant was not the first to recognize this, he was the first to make it the cornerstone of a fully worked-out system of morals.

But Kant went one step further and said that consistency requires rules that have no exceptions. One can see how his insight pushed him in that direction; but the extra step was not necessary, and it has caused trouble for his theory. Rules, even within a Kantian framework, need not be regarded as absolute. All that Kant's basic idea requires is that when we violate a rule, we do so for a reason that we would be willing for anyone to accept. In the Case of the Inquiring Murderer, this means that we may violate the rule against lying only if we would be willing for anyone to lie in the same circumstances. And most of us would readily agree to that.

President Truman could also say that anyone in his position would have been justified in dropping the bomb. Thus, even if Truman was wrong, Kant's arguments do not prove it. One might say, instead, that Truman was wrong because he had better options. Perhaps he should have tried negotiating with the Japanese before dropping the bomb. Saying *that*, however, is very different from saying that what Truman did violated an absolute rule.

CHAPTER 10

*K*ant and Respect for Persons

Are there any who would not admire man?

GIOVANNI PICO DELLA MIRANDOLA,
ORATION ON THE DIGNITY OF MAN (1486)

10.1. Kant's Core Ideas

Immanuel Kant thought that human beings occupy a special place in creation. Of course, he was not alone in thinking this. From ancient times, humans have considered themselves to be essentially different from all other creatures—and not just different, but better. In fact, humans have traditionally thought themselves to be quite fabulous. Kant certainly did. On his view, human beings have "an intrinsic worth" or "dignity" that makes them valuable "above all price."

Other animals, Kant thought, have value only insofar as they serve human purposes. In his *Lectures on Ethics* (1779), he writes, "But so far as animals are concerned, we have no direct duties. Animals . . . are there merely as means to an end. That end is man." We can, therefore, use animals in any way we please. We don't even have a "direct duty" to refrain from torturing them. Kant did condemn the torture of animals, but not because the animals would be hurt. He worried, rather, about us: "He who is cruel to animals also becomes hard in his dealings with men."

When Kant said that human beings are valuable "above all price," this was not mere rhetoric. Kant meant that people are irreplaceable. If a child dies, this is a tragedy, and it remains tragic even if another child is born into the same family. On the other hand, "mere things" are replaceable. If your printer breaks, then everything is fine so long as you can get another printer. People, Kant believed, have a "dignity" that mere things lack.

136

Two facts about people, on Kant's view, support this judgment.

First, because people have desires, things that satisfy those desires can have value *for* people. By contrast, "mere things" have value only insofar as they promote human ends. Thus, if you want to become a better poker player, a book about poker will have value for you; but apart from such ends, those books are worthless. Or, if you want to go somewhere, a car will have value for you; but apart from such desires, cars have no value.

Mere animals, Kant thought, are too primitive to have self-conscious desires and goals. Thus, they are "mere things." Kant did not believe, for example, that milk has value *for* the cat who wishes to drink it. But today we're more impressed with the mental life of animals than Kant was. We believe that animals do have desires and goals. So, perhaps there are Kantian grounds for saying that animals are not "mere things."

However, Kant's second reason would not apply to animals. People, Kant said, have "an intrinsic worth, i.e., dignity" because they are *rational agents,* that is, free agents capable of making their own decisions, setting their own goals, and guiding their conduct by reason. The only way that moral goodness can exist is for rational creatures *to act from a good will*—that is, to apprehend what they should do and act from a sense of duty. Human beings are the only rational agents that exist on earth; nonhuman animals lack free will, and they do not "guide their conduct by reason," because their rational capacities are too limited. If people disappeared, then so would the moral dimension of the world. This second fact about people is especially important for Kant.

It makes no sense, therefore, to regard human beings as merely one valuable thing among others. Humans are the ones who do the valuing, and it is their conscientious actions that have moral worth. Human beings tower above the realm of things.

These thoughts are central to Kant's morality. Kant believed that all of our duties can be derived from one ultimate principle, which he called the Categorical Imperative. Kant gave this principle different formulations, but at one point he expresses it like this:

> Act so that you treat humanity, whether in your own person or in that of another, always as an end and never as a means only.

Because people are so valuable, morality requires us to treat them "always as an end and never as a means only." What does this mean, and why should anyone believe it?

To treat people "as an end" means, on the most superficial level, treating them well. We must promote their welfare, respect their rights, avoid harming them, and generally "endeavor, so far as we can, to further the ends of others." But Kant's idea also has a deeper implication. To treat people as ends requires treating them with respect. Thus, we may not manipulate people, or use people to achieve our purposes, no matter how good those purposes may be. Kant gives this example: Suppose you need money, and you want a loan, but you know you cannot repay it. In desperation, you consider telling your friend you will repay it in order to get the money. May you do this? Perhaps you need the money for a good purpose—so good, in fact, that you might convince yourself that the lie would be justified. Nevertheless, you should not lie to your friend. If you did, you would be manipulating her and using her "merely as a means."

On the other hand, what would it be like to treat your friend "as an end"? Suppose you tell the truth—you tell her why you need the money, and you tell her you won't be able to pay her back. Then your friend can make up her own mind about whether to give you the loan. She can consult her own values and wishes, exercise her own powers of reasoning, and make a free choice. If she then decides to give you the money for your stated purpose, she will be choosing *to make that purpose her own.* Thus, you will not be using her as a mere means to achieving your goal, for it will be her goal, too. Thus, for Kant, to treat people as ends is to treat them "as beings who [can] contain in themselves the end of the very same action."

When you tell your friend the truth, and she gives you money, you are using her as a means to getting the money. However, Kant does not object to treating someone as a means; he objects to treating someone *only* as a means. Consider another example: Suppose your bathroom sink is stopped up. Would it be okay to call in a plumber—to "use" the plumber as a means to unclogging the drain? Kant would have no problem with this. The plumber, after all, understands the situation. You are not deceiving or manipulating him. He may freely choose to unclog your drain in exchange for payment. Although you are treating the plumber as a means, you are also treating him with dignity, as an "end-in-himself."

Treating people as ends, and respecting their rational capacities, has other implications. We should not force adults to do things against their will; instead, we should let them make their own decisions. We should therefore be wary of laws that aim to protect people from themselves—for example, laws requiring people to wear seat belts or motorcycle helmets. Also, we shouldn't forget that respecting *people* requires respecting *ourselves*. I should take good care of myself; I should develop my talents; I should do more than just slide by.

Kant's ethical system is not easy to grasp. To understand it better, let's consider how Kant applied his ideas to the practice of criminal punishment. The rest of this chapter is devoted to that example.

10.2. Retribution and Utility in the Theory of Punishment

Jeremy Bentham (1748–1832) said that "all punishment is mischief: all punishment in itself is evil." Bentham had a point. Punishment, by its nature, always involves inflicting some harm on the person punished. As a society, we punish people by making them pay fines or go to prison, or even, sometimes, by killing them. How can it be right to treat people in these ways?

The traditional answer is that punishment is justified as a way of "paying back" the offender for his wicked deed. Those who have committed a crime deserve to be treated badly. It is a matter of justice: If you harm other people, justice requires that you be harmed, too. As the ancient saying has it, "An eye for an eye, and a tooth for a tooth." According to the doctrine of Retributivism, this is the main justification of punishment.

Retributivism was, on Bentham's view, a wholly unsatisfactory idea, because it advocates the infliction of suffering without any compensating gain in happiness. Retributivism would have us increase, not decrease, the amount of misery in the world. Kant, a retributivist, openly embraced this implication of his view. In *The Critique of Practical Reason* (1788), he writes:

> When someone who delights in annoying and vexing peace-loving folk receives at last a right good beating, it is

certainly an ill, but everyone approves of it and considers
it as good in itself even if nothing further results from it.

Thus, punishing people may increase the amount of misery in
the world; but that is all right, for the extra suffering is borne
by those who deserve it.

Utilitarianism takes a very different approach. According
to Utilitarianism, our duty is to do whatever will increase the
amount of happiness in the world. Punishment is, on its face,
"an evil" because it makes the punished person unhappy. Thus,
Bentham, a utilitarian, says, "If [punishment] ought at all to
be admitted, it ought to be admitted in as far as it promises to
exclude some greater evil." In other words, punishment can be
justified only if it does enough good to outweigh the bad. And
utilitarians have traditionally thought that it does. If someone
breaks the law, then punishing that person can benefit society
in several ways.

First, punishment provides comfort and gratification to
victims and their families. People feel very strongly that someone who mugged, raped, or robbed them should not go free.
Victims also live in fear when they know that their attacker has
not been caught. Philosophers sometimes ignore this justification of punishment, but it plays a prominent role in our legal
system. Judges, lawyers, and juries often want to know what victims want. Indeed, whether the police will make an arrest, and
whether the district attorney's office will prosecute a case, often
depends on the wishes of the victims.

Second, by locking up criminals, or by executing them, we
take them off the street. With fewer criminals on the street, there
will be less crime. In this way, prisons protect society and thus
reduce unhappiness. Of course, this justification does not apply
to punishments in which the offender remains free, such as when
a criminal is sentenced to probation with community service.

Third, punishment reduces crime by deterring would-be
criminals. Someone who is tempted to commit a crime might
not do so if he knows he might be punished. Obviously, the
threat of punishment is not always effective; sometimes people
break the law anyway. But there will be *less* misconduct if punishments are threatened. Imagine what it would be like if the
police stopped arresting thieves; surely there would be a lot more
theft. And since criminal misconduct causes unhappiness to its
victims, in deterring crime we are preventing unhappiness.

Fourth, a well-designed system of punishment might help to rehabilitate wrongdoers. Criminals often have mental or emotional problems; they are often illiterate and uneducated and cannot hold down jobs. Why not respond to crime by attacking the problems that cause it? If someone is committing crimes, we may imprison him because he is dangerous. But while he is behind bars, his problems should be addressed with psychological therapy, educational opportunities, or job training, as appropriate. If one day he can return to society as a productive citizen, then both he and society will benefit.

In America, the utilitarian view of punishment was once dominant. In 1954, the American Prison Association changed its name to "the American Correctional Association" and encouraged prisons to become "correctional facilities." Prisons were thus asked to "correct" inmates, not to "punish" them. Prison reform was common in the 1950s and '60s. Hoping to turn inmates into good citizens, many prisons began offering drug treatment programs, vocational training classes, and group counseling sessions.

Those days, however, are long gone. In the 1970s, the newly announced "war on drugs" led to longer and longer prison sentences for drug offenders. This change in American justice was more retributive than utilitarian in nature, and it resulted in vastly more inmates—the American prison population has almost tripled in the last 20 years. Today more than 1 in 100 adults are behind bars, which amounts to a staggering 2.3 million inmates. At the same time, the states that must house all these prisoners are strapped for cash. As a result, most of the programs aimed at rehabilitation were either scaled back or eliminated. The rehabilitation mentality of the 1960s has thus been replaced by a warehousing mentality, marked by prison overcrowding and plagued by underfunding. This new reality, which is less pleasant for the inmates themselves, suggests a victory for Retributivism.

10.3. Kant's Retributivism

The utilitarian theory of punishment has many opponents. Some critics say that prison reform did not work. California had the most vigorous program of reform in the United States, yet its prisoners were especially likely to commit crimes after being released. Most of the opposition, however, is based on theoretical considerations that go back at least to Kant.

Kant despised "the serpent-windings of Utilitarianism" because, he said, the theory is incompatible with human dignity. In the first place, it has us calculating how to use people as means to an end, and this is not permissible. If we imprison the criminal in order to secure the well-being of society, we are merely using him for the benefit of others. This violates the fundamental rule that "one man ought never to be dealt with merely as a means subservient to the purpose of another."

Moreover, rehabilitation is really just the attempt to mold people into what *we* want them to be. As such, it violates their right to decide for themselves what sort of people they will be. We do have the right to respond to their wickedness by "paying them back" for it, but we do not have the right to violate their integrity by trying to manipulate their personalities.

Thus, Kant would have no part of utilitarian justifications for punishment. Instead, he argues that punishment should be governed by two principles. First, people should be punished simply because they have committed crimes, and for no other reason:

> Juridical punishment can never be administered merely as a means for promoting another good either with regard to the criminal himself or to civil society, but must in all cases be imposed only because the individual on whom it is inflicted has committed a crime.

And second, Kant says it is important to punish the criminal *proportionately* to the seriousness of his crime. Small punishments may suffice for small crimes, but big punishments are necessary for big crimes:

> But what is the mode and measure of punishment which public justice takes as its principle and standard? It is just the principle of equality, by which the pointer of the scale of justice is made to incline no more to the one side than to the other. . . . Hence it may be said: "If you slander another, you slander yourself; if you steal from another, you steal from yourself; if you strike another, you strike yourself; if you kill another, you kill yourself." This is . . . the only principle which . . . can definitely assign both the quality and the quantity of a just penalty.

Kant's second principle leads him to endorse capital punishment; for in response to murder, only death is appropriate. In a famous passage, Kant says:

> Even if a civil society resolved to dissolve itself with the consent of all its members—as might be supposed in the case of a people inhabiting an island resolving to separate and scatter throughout the whole world—the last murderer lying in prison ought to be executed before the resolution was carried out. This ought to be done in order that every one may realize the desert of his deeds, and that blood-guiltiness may not remain on the people; for otherwise they will all be regarded as participants in the murder as a public violation of justice.

Although a Kantian must support the death penalty *in theory*, she might oppose it *in practice*. The worry, in practice, is that innocent people might be killed by mistake. In the United States, around 130 death row inmates have been released from prison after being proved innocent. None of those people were actually killed. But with so many close calls, it is almost certain that some innocent people have been put to death—and advocates of reform point to specific, troubling examples. Thus, in deciding whether to support a policy of capital punishment, Kantians must balance the injustice of the occasional mistake against the injustice of a system that lets convicted killers continue to live.

Kant's two principles describe a general theory of punishment: Wrongdoers must be punished, and the punishment must fit the crime. This theory is deeply opposed to the Christian idea of turning the other cheek. In the Sermon on the Mount, Jesus avows, "You have heard that it was said, 'An eye for an eye and a tooth for a tooth.' But I say to you, Do not resist the one who is evil. But if anyone slaps you on the right cheek, turn to him the other also." For Kant, such a response to evil is not only imprudent, but unjust.

What arguments can be given for Kant's view? We noted that Kant regards punishment as a matter of justice. He says that, if the guilty are not punished, justice is not done. That is one argument. But Kant also provides another argument, based on his conception of treating people as "ends-in-themselves." This additional argument is Kant's contribution to the theory of Retributivism.

On the face of it, it seems unlikely that we could describe punishing someone as "respecting him as a person" or as "treating him as an end." How could sending someone to prison be a way of respecting him? Even more paradoxically, how could executing someone be a way of treating him with dignity? For Kant, treating someone "as an end" means treating him as a rational being, who is responsible for his behavior. So now we may ask: What does it mean to be a responsible being?

Consider, first, what it means *not* to be such a being. Mere animals, who lack reason, are not responsible for their actions; nor are people who are mentally ill and not in control of themselves. In such cases, it would be absurd to "hold them accountable." We could not properly feel gratitude or resentment toward them, because they are not responsible for any good or ill they cause. Moreover, we cannot expect them to understand *why* we treat them as we do, any more than they understand why they behave as they do. So we have no choice but to deal with them by manipulating them, rather than by treating them as rational individuals. When we scold a dog for eating off the table, for example, we are merely trying to "train" him.

On the other hand, a rational being can freely decide what to do, based on his own conception of what is best. Rational beings *are* responsible for their behavior, and so they are accountable for what they do. We may feel gratitude when they behave well and resentment when they behave badly. Reward and punishment—not "training" or other manipulation—are the natural expressions of gratitude and resentment. Thus, in punishing people, we are holding them responsible for their actions in a way in which we cannot hold mere animals responsible. We are responding to them not as people who are "sick" or who have no control over themselves, but as people who have freely chosen their evil deeds.

Furthermore, in dealing with responsible agents, we may properly allow their conduct to determine, at least in part, how we respond to them. If someone has been kind to you, you may respond by being generous; and if someone is nasty to you, you may take that into account in deciding how to deal with him or her. And why shouldn't you? Why should you treat everyone alike, regardless of how *they* have chosen to behave?

Kant gives this last point a distinctive twist. There is, on his view, a deep reason for responding to other people "in kind."

When we choose to do something, after consulting our own values, we are in effect saying *this is the sort of thing that should be done.* In Kant's terminology, we are implying that our conduct be made into a "universal law." Therefore, when a rational being decides to treat people in a certain way, he decrees that in his judgment *this is the way people are to be treated.* Thus, if we treat him the same way in return, we are doing nothing more than treating him *as he has decided that people are to be treated.* If he treats others badly, and we treat him badly, we are complying with his own decision. We are, in a perfectly clear sense, respecting his judgment, by allowing it to control how we treat him. Thus, Kant says of the criminal, "His own evil deed draws the punishment upon himself."

This last argument can certainly be questioned. Why should we adopt the criminal's principle of action, rather than follow our own principles? Shouldn't we try to be "better than he is"? At the end of the day, what we think of Kant's theory may depend on how we view criminal behavior. If we see lawbreakers as victims of circumstance, who do not ultimately control their own actions, then the utilitarian model will have great appeal for us. In fact, Kant himself would insist that if criminals are not responsible agents, then it makes no sense to resent them and punish them. But to the extent that we view criminals as rational agents who freely choose to do harm, Kantian Retributivism will have great persuasive power.

CHAPTER 11

Feminism and the Ethics of Care

> But it is obvious that the values of women differ very often from the values which have been made by the other sex; naturally, this is so. Yet it is the masculine values that prevail.
> VIRGINIA WOOLF, *A ROOM OF ONE'S OWN* (1929)

11.1. Do Women and Men Think Differently about Ethics?

The idea that women and men think differently has traditionally been used to justify discrimination against women. Aristotle said that women are not as rational as men, and so they are naturally ruled by men. Immanuel Kant agreed, adding that women "lack civil personality" and should have no voice in public life. Jean-Jacques Rousseau tried to put a good face on this by emphasizing that women and men merely possess different virtues; but, of course, it turned out that men's virtues fit them for leadership, whereas women's virtues fit them for home and hearth.

Against this background, it is not surprising that the women's movement of the 1960s and '70s denied that women and men differ psychologically. The conception of men as rational and women as emotional was dismissed as a mere stereotype. Nature makes no mental or moral distinction between the sexes, it was said; and when there seem to be differences, it is only because women have been conditioned by an oppressive system to behave in "feminine" ways.

These days, however, most feminists believe that women do think differently than men. But, they add, women's ways of thinking are not inferior to men's, nor do the differences justify any kind of prejudice. On the contrary, female ways of thinking yield insights that have been missed in male-dominated areas. Thus, by attending to the distinctive approach of women, we can make progress in subjects that were stalled. Ethics is said to be a leading candidate for this treatment.

Kohlberg's Stages of Moral Development. Consider the following problem, devised by the educational psychologist Lawrence Kohlberg (1927–1987). Heinz's wife was near death, and her only hope was a drug that had been discovered by a pharmacist who was now selling it for an exorbitant price. The drug cost $200 to make, and the pharmacist was selling it for $2000. Heinz could raise only half of that. The pharmacist said that half wasn't enough, and when Heinz promised to pay the rest later, the pharmacist still refused. In desperation, Heinz considered stealing the drug. Would stealing the drug be wrong?

This problem, known as "Heinz's Dilemma," was used by Kohlberg in studying the moral development of children. Kohlberg interviewed children of various ages, presenting them with a series of dilemmas and asking them questions designed to reveal their thinking. Analyzing their responses, Kohlberg concluded that there are six stages of moral development. In these stages, the child or adult conceives of "right" in terms of

obeying authority and avoiding punishment (stage 1);

satisfying one's own desires and letting others do the same, through fair exchanges (stage 2);

cultivating one's relationships and performing the duties of one's social roles (stage 3);

obeying the law and maintaining the welfare of the group (stage 4);

upholding the basic rights and values of one's society (stage 5);

abiding by abstract, universal moral principles (stage 6).

So, if all goes well, we begin life with a self-centered desire to avoid punishment, and we end life with a set of abstract moral principles. Kohlberg, however, believed that only a small minority of adults make it to stage 5.

Heinz's Dilemma was presented to an 11-year-old boy named Jake, who thought it was obvious that Heinz should steal the drug. Jake explained:

> For one thing, a human life is worth more than money, and if the druggist only makes $1,000, he is still going to live, but if Heinz doesn't steal the drug, his wife is going to die.
>
> *(Why is life worth more than money?)*
>
> Because the druggist can get a thousand dollars later from rich people with cancer, but Heinz can't get his wife again.
>
> *(Why not?)*
>
> Because people are all different and so you couldn't get Heinz's wife again.

But Amy, also 11, saw the matter differently. Should Heinz steal the drug? Compared to Jake, Amy seems hesitant and evasive:

> Well, I don't think so. I think there might be other ways besides stealing it, like if he could borrow the money or make a loan or something, but he really shouldn't steal the drug—but his wife shouldn't die either. . . . If he stole the drug, he might save his wife then, but if he did, he might have to go to jail, and then his wife might get sicker again, and he couldn't get more of the drug, and it might not be good. So, they should really just talk it out and find some other way to make the money.

The interviewer asks Amy further questions, but she will not budge; she refuses to accept the terms in which the problem is posed. Instead, she recasts the issue as a conflict between Heinz and the pharmacist that must be resolved by further discussions.

In terms of Kohlberg's stages, Jake seems to have advanced beyond Amy. Amy's response is typical of people operating at stage 3, where personal relationships are paramount—Heinz and the pharmacist must work things out between them. Jake, on the other hand, appeals to impersonal principles—"a human life is worth more than money." Jake is operating at one of the later stages.

Gilligan's Objection. Kohlberg began studying moral development in the 1950s. Back then, psychologists almost always studied behavior rather than thought processes, and psychological researchers were thought of as men in white coats who watched rats run through mazes. Kohlberg's humanistic, cognitive approach pursued knowledge in a more appealing way. However, his central idea was flawed. It is legitimate to study how people think at different ages—if children think differently at ages 5, 10, and 15, that is certainly worth knowing. It is also worthwhile to identify the best ways of thinking. But these projects are different. One involves observing how children, in fact, think; the other involves assessing ways of thinking as better or worse. Different kinds of evidence are relevant to each investigation, and there is no reason to assume in advance that the results will match. Contrary to the opinion of older people, it *could* turn out that age does not bring wisdom.

Kohlberg's theory has also been criticized from a feminist perspective. In 1982, Carol Gilligan wrote a book called *In a Different Voice,* in which she objects to what Kohlberg says about Jake and Amy. The two children think differently, she says, but Amy's way of thinking is not inferior. When confronted with Heinz's Dilemma, Amy responds in typical female fashion to the personal aspects of the situation, whereas Jake, thinking like a male, sees only "a conflict between life and property that can be resolved by a logical deduction." Jake's response will be judged "at a higher level" only if one assumes, as Kohlberg does, that an ethic of principle is superior to an ethic of intimacy and caring. But why should we assume that? Admittedly, most moral philosophers have favored an ethic of principle, but that may be because most moral philosophers have been men.

The "male way of thinking"—the appeal to impersonal principles—abstracts away the details that give each situation its special flavor. Women, Gilligan says, find it harder to ignore those details. Amy worries, "If [Heinz] stole the drug, he might save his wife then, but if he did, he might have to go to jail, and then his wife might get sicker again, and he couldn't get more of the drug. . . ." Jake, who reduces the situation to "a human life is worth more than money," ignores all this.

Gilligan suggests that women's basic moral orientation is one of caring: "taking care" of others in a personal way, not just being concerned for humanity in general. This explains why Amy's response seems, at first, confused and uncertain. Sensitivity to the needs of others leads women to "attend to voices other than their own and to include in their judgment other points of view." Thus, Amy could not simply reject the pharmacist's point of view; rather, she wanted to talk to him and try to accommodate him. According to Gilligan, "Women's moral weakness, manifest in an apparent diffusion and confusion of judgment, is thus inseparable from women's moral strength, an overriding concern with relationships and responsibilities."

Other feminist thinkers have taken up this theme and developed it into a distinctive view about the nature of ethics. Virginia Held sums up the central idea: "Caring, empathy, feeling with others, being sensitive to each other's feelings, all may be better guides to what morality requires in actual contexts than may abstract rules of reason, or rational calculation, or at least they may be necessary components of an adequate morality."

Before discussing this idea, we may pause to consider how "feminine" it really is. Is it true that women and men think differently about ethics? And if it is true, what accounts for the difference?

Is It True That Women and Men Think Differently? Since Gilligan's book appeared, psychologists have conducted hundreds of studies on gender, the emotions, and morality. These studies reveal some differences between women and men. Women tend to score higher than men on tests that measure empathy. Also, brain scans reveal that women have a lower tendency than men to enjoy seeing people punished who have treated them unfairly—perhaps because women empathize even with those who have wronged them. Finally, women seem to care more about close personal relationships, whereas men care more about larger networks of shallow relationships. As Roy Baumeister put it, "Women specialize in the narrow sphere of intimate relationships. Men specialize in the larger group."

Women and men probably do think differently about ethics. These differences, however, cannot be very great. It is not as though women make judgments that are incomprehensible to men, or vice versa. Men can understand the value of caring relationships, even if they have to be reminded sometimes; and they can agree with Amy that the happiest solution to Heinz's Dilemma would be for the two men to work it out. For their part, women will hardly disagree that human life is worth more than money. And when we look at individuals, we find that some men are especially caring, and some women rely heavily on abstract principles. Plainly, the two sexes do not inhabit different moral universes. One scholarly article reviewed 180 studies and found that women are only slightly more care-oriented than men, and men are only slightly more justice-oriented than women. Even this watered-down conclusion, however, invites the question: Why should women be, on average, more caring than men?

There seem to be two possibilities. On the one hand, we might look for a social explanation. Perhaps women care more because of the social roles they occupy. Traditionally, women have been expected to do the housework and take care of the children; even if this expectation is sexist, the fact remains that women often stay home and raise the kids. It is easy to see how taking care of a family could lead one to adopt an ethic of care. Thus, the care perspective could be part of the psychological conditioning that girls receive.

On the other hand, we might seek a genetic explanation. Some differences between males and females show up at a very early age. One-year-old girls will spend more time looking at a film of a face than a film of cars, whereas one-year-old boys prefer the cars. Even one-day-old girls, but not one-day-old boys, will spend more time looking at a friendly face than looking at a mechanical object of the same size. This suggests that females might naturally be more social than males. If this were true, why would it be true?

Charles Darwin's theory of evolution might provide some insight. We may think of the Darwinian "struggle for survival" as a competition to get the maximum number of one's genes into the next generation. Traits that help accomplish this will be preserved in future generations, while traits that work against this goal will tend to disappear. In the 1970s, researchers in the field of Evolutionary Psychology began applying these ideas to human psychology. The idea is that people today have the emotions and behavioral tendencies that enabled their ancestors to reproduce in the distant past.

From this point of view, the key difference between males and females is that men can father thousands of children, while women can give birth only once every nine and a half months, until menopause. This means that males and females have different reproductive strategies. For men, the optimum strategy is to impregnate as many women as possible. Having done that, the man cannot devote much time to any particular child. For women, the optimum strategy is to invest heavily in each child and to have sex only with those men who are willing to stick around. This creates a tension between men and women, and it might explain why the sexes have evolved different attitudes. It explains, notoriously, why men have a greater sex drive than women. It also explains why women might be more attracted than men to the values of the nuclear family—in particular, to the value of caring.

This kind of explanation is often misunderstood. The point is not that people consciously calculate how to propagate their genes; no one does that. Nor is the point that people *should* calculate in this way; from an ethical point of view, they should not. The point is to explain what we observe.

11.2. Implications for Moral Judgment

Not all female philosophers are feminists, and not all feminists embrace the ethics of care. Nonetheless, the ethics of care is closely identified with modern feminist philosophy. As Annette Baier (1929–) puts it, "'Care' is the new buzzword."

One way of understanding an ethical view is to ask what difference it would make in practice. Does an ethic of care have different implications than a "male" approach to ethics? Here are three examples.

Family and Friends. Traditional theories of obligation are notoriously ill-suited to describing life among family and friends. Those theories take the notion of obligation as morally fundamental—they say what we *ought* to do. But, as Baier observes, when we try to construe "being a loving parent" as a duty, we encounter problems. A loving parent is motivated by love, not by duty. If parents care for their children only because they feel it is their duty, the children will sense it and realize they are unloved.

Moreover, the ideas of equality and impartiality that pervade theories of obligation seem deeply antagonistic to the values of love and friendship. John Stuart Mill said that a moral agent must be "as strictly impartial as a disinterested and benevolent spectator." But that is not the standpoint of a parent or friend. We do not regard our family and friends merely as members of the great crowd of humanity; we think of them as special.

The ethics of care, on the other hand, is perfectly suited to describe such relations. The ethics of care does not take "obligation" as fundamental; nor does it require that we impartially promote the interests of everyone alike. Instead, it begins with a conception of moral life as a network of relationships with specific people, and it sees "living well" as caring for those people, attending to their needs, and maintaining their trust.

These outlooks lead to different judgments about what we may do. May I devote my time and resources to caring for my friends and family, even if this means ignoring the needs of other people? From an impartial point of view, our duty is to promote the interests of everyone alike. But few of us accept that view. The ethics of care confirms the priority that we naturally give to our family and friends, and so it seems more plausible than an ethic of principle. Of course, it is not surprising that the ethics of care appears to do a good job of explaining the nature of our moral relations with friends and family. After all, those relationships are its primary inspiration.

Children with HIV. More than two million children under the age of 15 have HIV, the virus that causes AIDS. Right now only 10% of those children get decent medical care, while only 11% of pregnant women who have HIV are taking steps to protect their unborn children. Organizations such as UNICEF work to improve these numbers, but they never have enough money. By contributing to their work, we could save many lives.

A traditional ethic of principle, such as Utilitarianism, would conclude from this that we have a substantial duty to support UNICEF. The reasoning is straightforward: Almost all of us spend money on luxuries. Luxuries are not as important as protecting children from AIDS. Therefore, we should give at least some of our money to UNICEF. Of course, this argument can become complicated if we try to fill in all the details. But the basic idea is clear enough.

One might think that an ethic of care would reach a similar conclusion—after all, shouldn't we care for those disadvantaged children? But that misses the point. An ethic of care focuses on small-scale, personal relationships. If there is no such relationship, "caring" cannot take place. Nel Noddings (1929–) explains that the caring relation can exist only if the "cared-for" can interact with the "one-caring." At a minimum, the cared-for must be able to receive and acknowledge the care in a personal, one-to-one encounter. Otherwise, there is no obligation: "We are not obliged to act as one-caring if there is no possibility of completion in the other." Thus, Noddings concludes that we have no obligation to help "the needy in the far regions of the earth."

Many feminists regard Noddings's view as too extreme. Making personal relationships the whole of ethics, as she does, seems as wrong-headed as ignoring them altogether. A better approach might be to say that the ethical life includes both caring relationships *and* a benevolent concern for people generally. Our obligation to support UNICEF might then be seen as arising from our obligations of benevolence. If we take this approach, we may interpret the ethics of care as *supplementing* traditional theories rather than replacing them. Annette Baier seems to have this in mind when she writes that, eventually, "women theorists will need to connect their ethics of love with what has been the men theorists' preoccupation, namely, obligation."

Animals. Do we have obligations to nonhuman animals? Should we, for example, be vegetarians? One argument from an ethic of principle says that we should, because the business of raising and slaughtering animals for food causes them great suffering, and we could nourish ourselves without the cruelty. Since the modern animal rights movement began in the 1970s, this sort of argument has persuaded many people to stop eating meat.

Noddings suggests that this is a good issue "to test the basic notions on which an ethic of caring rests." What are those basic notions? First, such an ethic appeals to intuition and feeling rather than to principle. This leads to a different conclusion about vegetarianism, for most people do not feel that eating meat is wrong or that the suffering of livestock is important.

Noddings observes that our emotional responses to humans are different from our responses to animals.

A second "basic notion on which an ethic of caring rests" is the primacy of personal relationships. As we have noted, the cared-for in these relationships must be able to participate by responding to the care. Noddings believes that people do have this sort of relationship with their pets, and this can be the basis of an obligation:

> When one is familiar with a particular animal family, one comes to recognize its characteristic form of address. Cats, for example, lift their heads and stretch toward the one they are addressing. . . . When I enter my kitchen in the morning and my cat greets me from her favorite spot on the counter, I understand her request. This is the spot where she sits and "speaks" in her squeaky attempt to communicate her desire for a dish of milk.

A relationship is established, and the attitude of care must be summoned. But one has no such relationship with the cow in the slaughterhouse, and so, Noddings concludes, we have no obligation to do anything for the cow's sake.

What are we to make of this? If we use this issue "to test the basic notions on which an ethic of caring rests," does the ethic pass or fail the test? The opposing arguments are impressive. First, intuition and feeling are not reliable guides—at one time, people's intuitions told them that slavery was acceptable and that the subordination of women to men was God's plan. And second, whether the animal is in a position to respond "personally" to you may have a lot to do with the satisfaction you get from helping, but it has nothing to do with the animal's needs. Similarly, whether a faraway child would suffer from having AIDS has nothing to do with whether she can thank you personally for helping her avoid infection. These arguments, of course, appeal to principles that are said to be typical of male reasoning. Therefore, if the ethic of care is taken to be the whole of morality, such arguments will be ignored. On the other hand, if caring is only one part of morality, the arguments from principle still have considerable force. Livestock might come within the sphere of moral concern, not because of our caring relation with them, but for other reasons.

11.3. Implications for Ethical Theory

It is easy to see the influence of men's experience in the ethical theories they have created. Historically, men have dominated public life, where relationships are often impersonal and contractual. In politics and business, relationships can even be adversarial when interests collide. So we negotiate; we bargain and make deals. Moreover, in public life, our decisions may affect large numbers of people we do not even know. So we may try to calculate which decisions will have the best overall outcome for the most people. And what do men's moral theories emphasize? Impersonal duty, contracts, the balancing of competing interests, and the calculation of costs and benefits.

Little wonder, then, that feminists believe that moral philosophy incorporates a male bias. The concerns of private life are almost wholly absent, and the "different voice" of which Carol Gilligan speaks is silent. A moral theory tailored to women's concerns would look very different. In the small-scale world of friends and family, bargaining and calculating play a much smaller role, while love and caring dominate. Once this point is made, there is no denying that morality must find a place for it.

Private life, however, is not easy to accommodate within the traditional theories. As we noted, "being a loving parent" is not about calculating how one should behave. The same might be said about being a loyal friend or a dependable coworker. To be loving, loyal, and dependable is to be *a certain kind of person,* which is very different from impartially "doing your duty."

The contrast between "being a certain kind of person" and "doing one's duty" lies at the heart of a larger conflict between two kinds of ethical theory. Virtue Theory sees being a moral person as having certain traits of character: being kind, generous, courageous, just, prudent, and so on. Theories of obligation, on the other hand, emphasize impartial duty: They portray the moral agent as someone who listens to reason, figures out the right thing to do, and does it. One of the chief arguments for Virtue Theory is that it seems well suited to accommodate the values of both public and private life. The two spheres require different virtues. Public life requires justice and beneficence, while private life requires love and caring.

The ethics of care, therefore, is best understood as one part of the ethics of virtue. Many feminist philosophers view it in this light. Although Virtue Theory is not exclusively a feminist project, it is so closely tied to feminist ideas that Annette Baier dubs its male promoters "honorary women." The verdict on the ethics of care will depend, ultimately, on the viability of a broader theory of the virtues.

CHAPTER 12

The Ethics of Virtue

> The concepts of obligation and duty—*moral* obligation and *moral* duty, that is to say—and of what is *morally* right and wrong, and of the *moral* sense of "ought," ought to be jettisoned. . . . It would be a great improvement if, instead of "morally wrong," one always named a genus such as "untruthful," "unchaste," "unjust."
>
> ELIZABETH ANSCOMBE, "MODERN MORAL PHILOSOPHY" (1958)

12.1. The Ethics of Virtue and the Ethics of Right Action

In thinking about any subject, it matters greatly what questions we begin with. In Aristotle's *Nicomachean Ethics* (ca. 325 B.C.), the central questions are about *character*. Aristotle begins by asking "What is the good of man?" and his answer is "an activity of the soul in conformity with virtue." He then discusses such virtues as courage, self-control, generosity, and truthfulness. Most of the ancient thinkers came to ethics by asking *What traits of character make someone a good person?* As a result, "the virtues" occupied center stage in their discussions.

As time passed, however, this way of thinking came to be neglected. With the coming of Christianity, a new set of ideas emerged. The Christians, like the Jews, viewed God as a lawgiver, and for them, righteous living meant obedience to the divine commandments. For the Greeks, the life of virtue was inseparable from the life of reason. But Saint Augustine, the influential fourth-century Christian thinker, distrusted reason and taught that moral goodness depends on subordinating oneself to the will of God. Therefore, when the medieval philosophers discussed the virtues, it was in the context of Divine Law. The "theological virtues" of faith, hope, charity, and obedience came to have a central place.

158

After the Renaissance Period (1400–1650), moral philosophy again became more secular, but philosophers did not return to the Greek way of thinking. Instead, the Divine Law was replaced by something called the "Moral Law." The Moral Law, which was said to spring from human reason rather than from God, was conceived to be a system of rules specifying which actions are right. Our duty as moral persons, it was said, is to follow those rules. Thus, modern moral philosophers approached their subject by asking a fundamentally different question from the one asked by the ancients. Instead of asking *What traits of character make someone a good person?* they began by asking *What is the right thing to do?* This led them in a different direction. They went on to develop theories, not of virtue, but of rightness and obligation:

- *Ethical Egoism:* Each person ought to do whatever will best promote his or her own interests.
- *The Social Contract Theory:* The right thing to do is to follow the rules that rational, self-interested people would agree to follow for their mutual benefit.
- *Utilitarianism:* One ought to do whatever will make everyone the happiest.
- *Kant's theory:* Our duty is to follow rules that we could accept as universal laws—that is, rules that we would be willing for everyone to follow in all circumstances.

And these are the theories that have dominated moral philosophy from the 17th century on.

Should We Return to the Ethics of Virtue? Recently, however, a number of philosophers have advanced a radical idea. Moral philosophy, they say, is bankrupt, and we should return to Aristotle's way of thinking.

This was suggested fifty years ago by Elizabeth Anscombe in her article "Modern Moral Philosophy." Anscombe thinks that modern moral philosophy is misguided because it rests on the incoherent notion of a "law" without a lawgiver. The very concepts of obligation, duty, and rightness are inseparable from this self-contradictory notion. Therefore, she says, we should stop thinking about obligation, duty, and rightness, and return to Aristotle's approach. The virtues should once again take center stage.

In the wake of Anscombe's article, a flood of books and essays appeared discussing the virtues, and Virtue Theory soon became a major option in contemporary ethics. A common set of concerns motivates this approach. In what follows, we will first take a look at what Virtue Theory is like. Then we will consider some reasons for preferring this theory to other, more modern ways of approaching the subject. Finally, we will consider whether a return to Virtue Theory is a viable option.

12.2. The Virtues

A theory of virtue should have several components: a statement of what a virtue is, a list of the virtues, an account of what these virtues consist in, and an explanation of why these qualities are good for a person to have. In addition, the theory should tell us whether the virtues are the same for all people or whether they differ from person to person or from culture to culture.

What Is a Virtue? Aristotle said that a virtue is a trait of character manifested in habitual action. The word "habitual" here is important. The virtue of honesty, for example, is not possessed by someone who tells the truth only occasionally or only when it benefits her. The honest person is truthful as a matter of course; her actions "spring from a firm and unchangeable character."

But this does not distinguish virtues from vices, for vices are also traits of character manifested in habitual action. The other part of the definition is evaluative: virtues are good, whereas vices are bad. Thus, a virtue is a *commendable* trait of character manifested in habitual action. Saying this, of course, doesn't tell us which traits of character are good or bad. Later we will flesh this out by discussing some ways in which the virtues are good. For now, we might note that virtuous qualities are those qualities that will make us seek out someone's company. As Edmund L. Pincoffs (1919–1991) put it, "Some sorts of persons we prefer; others we avoid. The properties on our list [of virtues and vices] can serve as reasons for preference or avoidance."

We seek out people for different purposes, and this affects which virtues are relevant. In looking for an auto mechanic, we want someone who is skillful, honest, and conscientious; in looking for a teacher, we want someone who is knowledgeable, articulate, and patient. Thus, the virtues of auto repair are different from the virtues of teaching. But we also assess people *as people,* in a more general way, so we have the concept, not just of a good mechanic or a good teacher, but of a good person. The moral virtues are the virtues of persons as such. Thus, we may define a moral virtue as *a trait of character, manifested in habitual action, that it is good for anyone to have.*

What Are the Virtues? What, then, are the virtues? Which traits of character should be fostered in human beings? There is no short answer, but the following is a partial list:

benevolence	fairness	patience
civility	friendliness	prudence
compassion	generosity	reasonableness
conscientiousness	honesty	self-discipline
cooperativeness	industriousness	self-reliance
courage	justice	tactfulness
courteousness	loyalty	thoughtfulness
dependability	moderation	tolerance

The list could be expanded, of course.

What Do These Virtues Consist In? It is one thing to say, in general, that we should be conscientious, compassionate, and tolerant; it is another thing to say exactly what these character traits consist in. Each of the virtues has its own distinctive features and raises its own distinctive problems. We will look briefly at four of them.

1. *Courage.* According to Aristotle, virtues are midpoints between extremes: A virtue is "the mean by reference to two vices: the one of excess and the other of deficiency." Courage is a mean between the extremes of cowardice and foolhardiness—it is cowardly to run away from all danger, yet it is foolhardy to risk too much.

Courage is sometimes said to be a military virtue because soldiers so obviously need to have it. But soldiers are not the only ones who need courage. We all need courage, and not just when we face a pre-existing danger, such as an enemy soldier or a grizzly bear. Sometimes we need the courage to *create* a situation that will be unpleasant for us. It takes courage to apologize. If a friend is grieving, it takes courage to ask her directly how she is doing. It takes courage to volunteer to do something nice that you don't really want to do.

If we consider only ordinary cases, the nature of courage seems unproblematic. But unusual circumstances present more troublesome cases. Consider the 19 hijackers who murdered almost 3000 people on September 11, 2001. They faced certain death, evidently without flinching, but in the service of an evil cause. Were they courageous? The American political commentator Bill Maher implied that they were—and so he lost his television show, *Politically Incorrect*. The philosopher Peter Geach, however, disagrees. "Courage in an unworthy cause," he says, "is no virtue; still less is courage in an evil cause. Indeed I prefer not to call this nonvirtuous facing of danger 'courage.'"

It is easy to see Geach's point. Calling a terrorist "courageous" seems to praise his performance, and we do not want to do that. But, on the other hand, it doesn't seem quite right to say that he is *not* courageous—after all, look at how he behaves in the face of danger. To get around this problem, perhaps we should just say that he displays two qualities of character, one admirable (steadfastness in facing danger) and one detestable (a willingness to kill innocent people). He is courageous, as Maher suggested, and courage is a good thing; but because his courage is deployed in such an evil cause, his behavior is *on the whole* extremely wicked.

2. *Generosity.* Generosity is the willingness to expend one's resources to help others. Aristotle says that generosity, like courage, is a mean between extremes: It falls between stinginess and extravagance. The stingy person gives too little; the extravagant person gives too much. But how much is enough?

Another ancient teacher, Jesus of Nazareth, said that we must give all we have to help the poor. Jesus found it unacceptable to possess riches while the poor starve. Those who heard him thought that this was a hard teaching to follow, and they generally rejected it. Today most people still reject this doctrine, even those who consider themselves to be Jesus's followers.

The modern utilitarians are, in this regard, Jesus's moral descendants. They hold that in every circumstance it is our duty to do whatever will have the best overall consequences for everyone concerned. This means that we should be generous with our money until the point at which further giving would be more harmful to us than it would be helpful to others.

Why do people resist this idea? Partly it may be due to selfishness; we do not want to make ourselves poor by giving away what we have. But also, adopting such a policy would prevent us from living normal lives. Not only money but time is involved; our lives consist in projects and relationships that require a considerable investment of both. An ideal of "generosity" that demands spending our money and time as Jesus and the utilitarians recommend would require us to abandon our everyday lives.

A reasonable interpretation of generosity might, therefore, be something like this: We should be as generous with our resources as we can be while still carrying on our normal lives. But even this interpretation will leave us with some awkward questions. Some people's "normal lives" are quite extravagant—think of a rich person who has grown accustomed to great luxuries. Surely such a person can't be generous unless he is willing to sell his yacht to feed the hungry. The virtue of generosity, it would seem, cannot exist in the context of a life that is too opulent. To make this interpretation of generosity "reasonable," we need a conception of normal life that is not too extravagant.

3. *Honesty.* The honest person is, first of all, someone who does not lie. But is that enough? There are other ways of misleading people than by lying. Geach tells the story of Saint Athanasius, who "was rowing on a river when the persecutors came rowing in the opposite direction: 'Where is the traitor Athanasius?' 'Not far away,' the Saint gaily replied, and rowed past them unsuspected."

Geach approves of Athanasius's deception even though he thinks it would have been wrong to tell an outright lie. Lying, Geach thinks, is always forbidden: A person possessing the virtue of honesty will not even consider it. Honest people will not lie, and so they will have to find other ways to deal with difficult situations. Athanasius was clever enough to do so. He told the truth, even if it was a deceptive truth. But it is hard to see why Athanasius's deception was not also dishonest. What plausible principle would approve of misleading people by one means but not by another?

Geach's example raises the question of whether virtue requires adherence to absolute rules. Concerning honesty, we may distinguish two views:

1. An honest person will never lie.
2. An honest person will never lie except in rare circumstances when there are compelling reasons to do so.

Why must we accept the first view? There is, in fact, good reason to favor the second. Consider why lying is a bad thing:

Our ability to live together in communities depends on our ability to communicate. We talk to one another, read each other's writing, exchange information and opinions, express our desires to one another, make promises, ask and answer questions, and much more. Without these sorts of exchanges, social living would be impossible. But for these exchanges to work, we must be able to rely on one another to speak honestly.

Moreover, when we take people at their word, we make ourselves vulnerable to them. By accepting what they say and modifying our beliefs and actions accordingly, we place our welfare in their hands. If they speak truthfully, all is well. But if they lie, we end up with false beliefs; and if we act on those beliefs, we end up doing foolish things. We trusted them, and they let us down. This explains why lying is offensive. It is at bottom a violation of trust. It also explains why lies and "deceptive truths" seem morally indistinguishable: Both violate trust in the same way.

None of this, however, implies that honesty is the only important value or that we must tell the truth to everyone who comes along, regardless of what they are up to. Suppose Saint Athanasius had told the persecutors, "I don't know who that is," and as a result, his pursuers went off on a wild goose chase. Later, could they have complained that the saint had violated their trust? No; they had forfeited their right to his honesty when they set out to persecute him unjustly. In such circumstances, self-preservation is more important than honesty.

4. *Loyalty to friends and family.* If we needed proof that humans are social creatures, the existence of friendship would supply all the proof we could want. As Aristotle says, "No one would choose to live without friends, even if he had all other goods":

> How could prosperity be safeguarded and preserved without friends? The greater our prosperity is, the greater are the risks it brings with it. Also, in poverty and all other kinds of misfortune men believe that their only refuge consists in their friends. Friends help young men avoid error; to older people they give the care and help needed to supplement the failing powers of action which infirmity brings.

The benefits of friendship, of course, go far beyond material assistance. Psychologically, we would be lost without our friends. Our triumphs seem hollow without friends to share them with, and we need our friends even more when we fail. Our self-esteem depends in large measure on the assurances of friends: By returning our affection, they confirm our worth as human beings.

If we need friends, then we need the qualities that enable us to *be* a friend. Near the top of the list is loyalty. Friends can be counted on. You stick by your friends even when things are going badly and even when, objectively speaking, you should abandon them. Friends make allowances for one another; they forgive offenses and refrain from harsh judgments. There are limits, of course—sometimes only a friend can tell us the hard truth about ourselves. But criticism is acceptable from friends because we know that they are not rejecting us.

None of this is to deny that we have duties to other people, even to strangers. But they are different duties, associated with different virtues. Generalized beneficence is a virtue, and it may demand a great deal, but it does not require the same level of concern for strangers as for friends. Justice is another such virtue; it requires impartial treatment for all. But friends are loyal to one another, so the demands of justice are weaker when friends are involved.

We are even closer to family members than we are to friends; so, we may show family members even more loyalty and partiality. In Plato's *Euthyphro*, Socrates learns that Euthyphro has come to the courthouse to prosecute his own father for murder. Socrates expresses surprise at this and wonders whether a son should bring charges against his father. Euthyphro sees no impropriety: For him, a murder is a murder. Euthyphro has a point, but we might still be shocked that someone could take the same attitude toward his father that he would take toward a stranger. A close family member, we might think, need not be involved in such a legal matter. This point is recognized in American law: In the United States, one cannot be compelled to testify in court against one's husband or wife.

Why Are the Virtues Important? We said that virtues are traits of character that are good for people to have. This raises the question of why the virtues are good. Why should a person be courageous, generous, honest, or loyal? The answer may depend on the virtue in question. Thus:

- Courage is good because we need it to cope with danger.
- Generosity is desirable because there will always be people who need help.

- Honesty is needed because without it relations between people would go wrong in all sorts of ways.
- Loyalty is essential to friendship; friends stand by one another even when they are tempted to turn away.

This list suggests that each virtue is valuable for a different reason. However, Aristotle offers a general answer to our question—namely, that the virtues are important because the virtuous person will fare better in life. The point is not that the virtuous will always be richer; the point is that we need the virtues in order to flourish.

To see what Aristotle is getting at, consider who we are and how we live. On the most general level, we are social creatures who want the company of others. So we live in communities among family, friends, and fellow citizens. In this setting, such qualities as loyalty, fairness, and honesty are needed to interact successfully with others. On a more individual level, we might have a job and pursue particular interests. Those activities might call for other virtues, such as perseverance and industriousness. Finally, it is part of our common human condition that we must sometimes face danger or temptation, so courage and self-control are needed. Thus, the virtues all have the same general sort of value: They are all qualities needed for successful living.

Are the Virtues the Same for Everyone? Finally, we may ask whether a single set of traits is desirable for all people. Should we speak of *the* good person, as though all good people come from one mold? This assumption has been challenged. Friedrich Nietzsche (1844–1900), for example, did not think that there is only one kind of human goodness. In his flamboyant way, Nietzsche observes:

> how naive it is altogether to say: "Man *ought* to be such-and-such!" Reality shows us an enchanting wealth of types, the abundance of a lavish play and change of forms—and some wretched loafer of a moralist comments: "No! Man ought to be different." He even knows what man should be like, this wretched bigot and prig: he paints himself on the wall and comments, *"Ecce homo!"* ["Behold the man!"]

There is obviously something to this. The scholar who devotes his life to understanding medieval literature and the professional soldier are very different kinds of people. A Victorian woman who would never expose a leg in public and a woman who sunbathes on a nude beach have very different standards of modesty. And yet all may be admirable in their own ways.

There is, then, an obvious sense in which the virtues may differ from person to person. Because people lead different kinds of lives, have different sorts of personalities, and occupy different social roles, the qualities of character that help them flourish may differ.

It is tempting to go even further and say that the virtues differ from society to society. After all, the kind of life that is possible will depend on the values and institutions that dominate a region. A scholar's life is possible only where there are institutions, such as universities, that make intellectual investigation possible. Much the same could be said about being an athlete, a priest, a geisha, or a samurai warrior. The character traits that are needed to occupy those roles will differ, and so the traits needed to live successfully will differ. Thus, the virtues will be different.

To this it may be answered that *certain virtues will be needed by all people in all times.* This was Aristotle's view, and he was probably right. Aristotle believed that we all have a great deal in common, despite our differences. "One may observe," he says, "in one's travels to distant countries the feelings of recognition and affiliation that link every human being to every other human being." Even in the most disparate societies, people face the same basic problems and have the same basic needs. Thus:

- Everyone needs courage, because no one (not even the scholar) can always avoid danger. Also, everyone needs the courage to take the occasional risk.
- In every society, there will be some people who are worse off than others; so generosity will always be prized.
- Honesty is always a virtue because no society can exist without dependable communication.
- Everyone needs friends, and to have friends one must be a friend; so everyone needs loyalty.

This sort of list could—and in Aristotle's hands it does—go on and on.

To summarize, then, it may be true that in different societies the virtues are given different interpretations, and different actions are counted as satisfying them; and it may be true that the value of a character trait will vary from person to person and from society to society. But it cannot be right to say that social customs determine whether any particular character trait is a virtue. The major virtues are mandated not by custom but by facts about our common human condition.

12.3. Two Advantages of Virtue Theory

Virtue Theory is often said to have two advantages over other theories.

1. *Moral motivation*. Virtue Theory is appealing because it provides a natural and attractive account of moral motivation. Consider the following:

You are in the hospital recovering from a long illness. You are bored and restless, and so you are delighted when Smith comes to visit. You have a good time talking to him; his visit is just what you needed. After a while, you tell Smith how much you appreciate his coming—he really is a good friend to take the trouble to come see you. But, Smith says, he is merely doing his duty. At first you think he is only being modest, but the more you talk, the clearer it becomes that he is speaking the literal truth. He is not visiting you because he wants to or because he likes you, but only because he thinks he should "do the right thing." He feels it is his duty to visit you, perhaps because he knows of no one else who is more in need of cheering up.

This example was suggested by the American philosopher Michael Stocker (1940–). As Stocker points out, you'd be very disappointed to learn Smith's motive; now his visit seems cold and calculating to you, and it loses its value. You thought he was your friend, but now you know otherwise. Commenting on Smith's behavior, Stocker says, "Surely there is something lacking here—and lacking in moral merit or value."

Of course, there is nothing wrong with *what* Smith did. The problem is *why* he did it. We value friendship, love, and respect, and we want our relationships to be based on mutual regard. Acting from an abstract sense of duty or from a desire to "do the right thing" is not the same. We would not want to live in a community of people who acted only from such motives, nor would we want to be such a person. Therefore, the argument goes, theories that focus on right action cannot provide a completely satisfactory account of the moral life. For that, we need a theory that emphasizes personal qualities such as friendship, love, and loyalty—in other words, a theory of the virtues.

2. *Doubts about the "ideal" of impartiality.* A dominant theme in modern moral philosophy has been impartiality—the idea that all persons are morally equal, and that we should treat everyone's interests as equally important. The utilitarian theory is typical. "Utilitarianism," John Stuart Mill writes, "requires [the moral agent] to be as strictly impartial as a disinterested and benevolent spectator." The book you are now reading also treats impartiality as a fundamental moral requirement: In the first chapter, impartiality was included in the "minimum conception" of morality.

It may be doubted, though, whether impartiality is really such a noble ideal. Consider our relationships with family and friends. Should we be impartial where their interests are concerned? A mother loves her children and cares for them in a way that she does not care for other children. She is partial to them through and through. But is anything wrong with that? Isn't that exactly the way a mother should be? Again, we love our friends, and we are willing to do things for them that we would not do for just anyone. What's wrong with that? Loving relationships are essential to the good life. But any theory that emphasizes impartiality will have a hard time accounting for this.

A moral theory that emphasizes the virtues, however, can easily account for all this. Some virtues are partial and some are not. Loyalty involves partiality toward loved ones and friends; beneficence involves equal regard for everyone. What is needed is not some general requirement of impartiality, but an understanding of these virtues and how they relate to one another.

12.4. Virtue and Conduct

As we have seen, theories that emphasize right action seem incomplete because they neglect the question of character. Virtue Theory remedies this problem by making character its central concern. But as a result, Virtue Theory runs the risk of being incomplete in the other direction. Moral problems are frequently problems about what to *do*. What can Virtue Theory tell us about the assessment, not of character, but of action?

The answer will depend on the spirit in which Virtue Theory is offered. On the one hand, we might combine the best features of the right action approach with insights drawn from the virtues approach—we might try to improve Utilitarianism or Kantianism, for example, by supplementing them with a theory of moral character. This seems sensible. If so, then we can assess right action simply by relying on Utilitarianism or Kantianism.

On the other hand, some writers believe that the ethics of virtue should be considered as an *alternative* to the other sorts of theories—as a complete moral theory in itself. We might call this "radical virtue ethics." What would such a theory say about right action? Either it will need to dispense with the notion of "right action" altogether, or it will have to give some account of the notion derived from the conception of virtuous character.

It might sound crazy, but some philosophers have argued that we should get rid of such concepts as "morally right action." Anscombe says that "it would be a great improvement" if we stopped using such notions. We could still assess conduct as better or worse, she says, but we would do so in other terms. Instead of saying that an action was "morally wrong," we would say that it was "intolerant" or "unjust" or "cowardly"—terms derived from the vocabulary of virtue. On her view, such terms allow us to say everything that we need to say.

But radical virtue ethicists need not reject notions such as "morally right." These ideas can be retained but given a new interpretation within the virtue framework. We could still judge actions based on the reasons that can be given for or against them. However, *the reasons cited will all be reasons connected with the virtues*. Thus, the reasons for doing some particular action might be that it is honest, or generous, or fair; while the reasons against doing it might be that it is dishonest, or stingy, or unfair. This analysis could be summed up by saying that the "right thing to do" is whatever a virtuous person would do.

12.5. The Problem of Incompleteness

The main problem for radical virtue ethics is the problem of incompleteness. The theory is incomplete in three ways.

First, it cannot explain everything it should explain. Consider a typical virtue, such as dependability. Why should I be dependable? Plainly, we need an answer to this question that goes beyond the simple observation that being dependable is a virtue. We want to know *why* dependability is a virtue; we want to know why it is good. Possible explanations might be that being dependable is to one's own advantage, or being dependable promotes the general welfare, or dependability is needed by those who must live together and rely on one another. The first explanation looks suspiciously like Ethical Egoism; the second is utilitarian; and the third recalls the Social Contract Theory. But none of these explanations are couched in terms of the virtues. Any explanation of why a particular virtue is good, it seems, would have to take us beyond the narrow confines of radical virtue ethics.

If radical virtue ethics doesn't explain *why* something is a virtue, then it won't be able to tell us whether the virtues apply to difficult cases. Consider the virtue of being beneficent, or being kind. Suppose I hear some news that would upset you to know about. Maybe I've learned that someone you used to know died in a car accident. If I don't tell you this, you might never find out. Suppose, also, that you're the sort of person who would want to be told. If I know all this, should I tell you the news? What would be the *kind* thing to do? It's a hard question, because what you would prefer—being told—conflicts with what would make you feel good—not being told. Would a kind person care more about what you want, or more about what makes you feel good? Radical virtue ethics cannot answer this question. To be kind is to look out for someone's best interests; but radical virtue ethics does not tell us what someone's best interests are. So, the second way in which the theory is incomplete is that it cannot give a full interpretation of the virtues. It cannot say exactly when they apply.

Finally, radical virtue ethics is incomplete because it cannot help us deal with cases of moral conflict. Suppose I just got a haircut—the same mullet I had in 1992—and I put you on the spot by asking you what you think. You can either tell me the truth, or you can say I look just fine. Honesty and kindness are both virtues, and so there are reasons both for and against each alternative. But you must do one or the other—you must either tell the truth and be unkind, or not tell the truth and be kind. Which should you do? If someone told you "Well, you should act virtuously in this situation," that wouldn't help you decide what to do; it would only leave you wondering which virtue to follow. Clearly, we need guidance beyond the resources of radical virtue ethics.

By itself, radical virtue ethics is limited to platitudes: be kind, be honest, be patient, be generous, and so on. Platitudes are vague, and by themselves they give us no guidance about what to do when they conflict with each other. Radical virtue ethics needs the resources of a larger theory.

12.6. Conclusion

It seems best to regard Virtue Theory as part of our overall theory of ethics rather than as being a complete theory in itself. The total theory would include an account of all the considerations that figure in practical decision making, together with their underlying rationales. The question is whether such a theory can accommodate both an adequate conception of right action and a related conception of virtuous character.

I don't see why not. Suppose, for example, that we accept a utilitarian theory of right action—we believe that one ought to do whatever will lead to the most happiness for everyone. From a moral point of view, we would want a society in which everyone leads happy and satisfying lives. We could then ask which actions, which social policies, *and which qualities of character* would most likely lead to that result. An inquiry into the nature of virtue could then be conducted from within that larger framework.

CHAPTER 13

*W*hat Would a Satisfactory Moral Theory Be Like?

Some people believe that there cannot be progress in Ethics, since everything has already been said. . . . I believe the opposite. . . . Compared with the other sciences, Non-Religious Ethics is the youngest and least advanced.

DEREK PARFIT, *REASONS AND PERSONS* (1984)

13.1. Morality without Hubris

Moral philosophy has a rich and fascinating history. Scholars have approached the subject from many different perspectives, producing theories that both attract and repel the thoughtful reader. Almost all the classical theories contain plausible elements, which is hardly surprising, since they were devised by philosophers of undoubted genius. Yet the various theories conflict with each other, and most of them are vulnerable to crippling objections. One is left wondering what to believe. What, in the final analysis, is the truth? Of course, different philosophers would answer this question in different ways. Some might refuse to give any answer, on the grounds that we do not know enough to have reached the "final analysis." In this respect, moral philosophy is not much worse off than any other subject of human inquiry—we do not know the final truth about most things. But we do know a lot, and it may not be rash to say something about what a satisfactory moral theory might be like.

A Modest Conception of Human Beings. A satisfactory theory would be realistic about where human beings fit in the grand scheme of things. The "big bang" occurred some 13.7 billion

173

years ago, and the earth was formed around 4.5 billion years ago. Life on earth evolved slowly, mostly according to the principles of natural selection. When the dinosaurs went extinct 65 million years ago, this left more room for the evolution of mammals, and a few hundred thousand years ago, one line of that evolution produced us. In geological time, we arrived only yesterday.

But no sooner did our ancestors arrive than they began to think of themselves as the crown of creation. Some of them even imagined that the whole universe had been made for their benefit. Thus, when they began to develop theories of right and wrong, they held that the protection of their own interests had a kind of ultimate and objective value. The rest of creation, they reasoned, was intended for their use. We now know better. We now know that we exist by evolutionary accident, as one species among millions, on one small speck in the unimaginably vast cosmos. The details of this picture are revised each year, as more is discovered, but the main outlines are well established. Some of the old story remains: we still believe that human beings are the smartest animals and the only ones that employ language. Those facts, however, cannot justify an entire worldview that places ourselves at the center.

How Reason Gives Rise to Ethics. Human beings have evolved as rational beings. Because we are rational, we are able to take some facts as reasons for behaving one way rather than another. We can articulate those reasons and think about them. Thus, if an action would help satisfy our desires, needs, and so on—in short, if it would *promote our interests*—then we take that as a reason to do it.

The origin of our concept of "ought" may be found in these facts. If we were incapable of considering reasons, we would have no use for such a notion. Like the other animals, we would act from instinct or habit. But the examination of reasons introduces a new factor. Now we find ourselves driven to act in certain ways as a result of deliberation, as a result of thinking about our behavior and its consequences. We use the word *ought* to mark this new element of the situation: We ought to do what there are the strongest reasons for doing.

Once we consider morality as a matter of acting on reason, another important point emerges. In reasoning about what to do, we can be consistent or inconsistent. One way of being inconsistent is to accept a fact as a reason on one occasion but to reject it as a reason on a similar occasion. This happens when one places the interests of one's own race above the interests of other races, despite the absence of any reason to do so. Racism is an offense against morality because it is an offense against reason. Similar remarks apply to other doctrines that divide humanity into the morally favored and disfavored, such as nationalism, sexism, and classism. The upshot is that reason requires impartiality: We ought to act so as to promote the interests of everyone alike.

If Psychological Egoism were true—if we could care only about ourselves—this would mean that reason demands more of us than we can manage. But Psychological Egoism is not true; it presents a false picture of human nature and the human condition. We have evolved as social creatures, living together in groups, wanting one another's company, needing one another's cooperation, and capable of caring about one another's welfare. So there is a pleasing "fit" between (a) what reason requires, namely, impartiality; (b) the requirements of social living, namely, adherence to rules that serve everyone's interests, if fairly applied; and (c) our natural inclination to care about others, at least to a modest degree. All three work together to make morality not only possible but *natural* for us.

13.2. Treating People as They Deserve

The idea that we should "promote the interests of everyone alike" is appealing when it is used to refute bigotry. However, sometimes there is good reason to treat people differently—sometimes people *deserve* to be treated better or worse than others. Human beings are rational agents who can make free choices. Those who choose to treat others well deserve good treatment; those who choose to treat others badly deserve ill treatment.

This sounds harsh until we consider examples. Suppose Smith has always been generous, helping you whenever she could, and now she is in trouble and needs your help. You now have a special reason to help her, beyond the general obligation you have to be helpful to everyone. She is not just a member of the great crowd of humanity; she has earned your respect and gratitude through her conduct.

By contrast, consider someone with the opposite history: Jones is your neighbor, and he has always refused to help you out. One day, for example, your car wouldn't start, and he wouldn't give you a ride to work—he just couldn't be bothered. Some time later, though, *he* has car trouble and asks *you* for a ride. Now Jones deserves to have to fend for himself. If you gave him a ride despite his past behavior, you would be choosing to treat him better than he deserves.

Treating people as they have chosen to treat others is not just a matter of rewarding friends and holding grudges against enemies. It is a matter of treating people as responsible agents who merit particular responses, based on their past conduct. There is an important difference between Smith and Jones: one of them deserves our gratitude; the other deserves our resentment. What would it be like if we did not care about such things?

For one thing, we would be denying people (including ourselves) the ability to earn good treatment at the hands of others. This is important. Because we live in communities, how each of us fares depends not only on what we do but on what others do as well. If we are to flourish, we need others to treat us well. A social system in which deserts are acknowledged gives us a way of doing that; it is a way of granting people the power to determine their own fates.

Absent this, what are we to do? What are the alternatives? We might imagine a system in which a person can get good treatment only by force, or by luck, or as a matter of charity. But the practice of acknowledging deserts is different. It gives people control over whether others will treat them well or badly. It says to them, "If you behave well, you will be *entitled* to good treatment from others. You will have earned it." Acknowledging deserts is ultimately a matter of "respect for persons" in a sense somewhat like Kant's.

13.3. A Variety of Motives

There are other ways in which the idea of "promoting the interests of everyone alike" apparently fails to capture the whole of moral life. (I say "apparently" because I want to return later to the question of whether the failure is apparent or real.) Certainly, people should sometimes be motivated by an impartial concern for "the interests of everyone alike." But there are other morally praiseworthy motives:

- A mother loves and cares for her children. She does not want to "promote their interests" simply because they are people she can help. Her attitude toward them is entirely different from her attitude toward other children. While she might feel that she should help other children when she can, that vaguely benevolent feeling is nothing like the love she has for her own.
- A man is loyal to his friends. Again, he is not concerned with their interests only as part of his concern for people generally. They are his friends, and so they are special to him.

Only a philosophical idiot would want to eliminate love, loyalty, and the like from our understanding of the moral life. If such motives were eliminated, and instead people simply calculated what was best, we would all be much worse off. And in any case, who would want to live in a world without love and friendship?

Of course, people may have many other valuable motives:

- A composer is concerned, above all else, to finish her symphony. She pursues this even though she might do "more good" by doing something else.
- A teacher devotes great effort to preparing his classes, even though more overall good might be accomplished if he directed part of this energy elsewhere.

While these motives are not usually considered "moral," we should not want to eliminate them from human life. Taking pride in one's job, wanting to create something of value, and many other noble intentions contribute to both personal happiness and the general welfare. We should no more want to eliminate them than to eliminate love and friendship.

13.4. Multiple-Strategies Utilitarianism

Above, I gave a sketchy justification of the principle that "we ought to act so as to promote the interests of everyone alike." But then I noted that this cannot be the whole story about our moral obligations because sometimes we should treat people differently, according to their individual deserts. And then I discussed some morally important motives that seem unrelated to the impartial promotion of interests.

Yet it may be possible to see these diverse concerns as inter-related. At first blush, it seems that treating people according to their individual deserts is quite different from seeking to promote the interests of everyone alike. But when we asked why deserts are important, the answer turned out to be that *we would all be much worse off* if acknowledging deserts was not part of our social scheme. And when we ask why love, friendship, artistic creativity, and pride in one's work are important, the answer is that *our lives would be so much poorer* without such things. This suggests that there is a single standard at work in our assessments.

Perhaps, then, the single moral standard is human welfare. What is important is that people be as happy as possible. And this standard can be used to assess a wide variety of things, including actions, policies, social customs, laws, rules, motives, and character traits. But this does not mean that we should always think in terms of making people as happy as possible. Our day-to-day lives will go better if, instead, we simply love our children, enjoy our friends, take pride in our work, keep our promises, and so on. An ethic that values "the interests of everyone alike" will endorse this conclusion.

This is not a new idea. Henry Sidgwick (1838–1900), the great utilitarian theorist of the Victorian era, made the same point:

> [T]he doctrine that Universal Happiness is the ultimate *standard* must not be understood to imply that Universal Benevolence is the only right or always best *motive* of action . . . it is not necessary that the end which gives the criterion of rightness should always be the end at which we consciously aim: and if experience shows that the general happiness will be more satisfactorily attained if men frequently act from other motives than pure universal philanthropy, it is obvious that these other motives are reasonably to be preferred on Utilitarian principles.

Sidgwick's thought has been cited in support of a view called "Motive Utilitarianism," which holds that we should act from the motives that best promote the general welfare.

Yet the most plausible view of this type does not focus exclusively on motives; nor does it focus entirely on acts or rules, as other theories have done. The most plausible view might be called *Multiple-Strategies Utilitarianism.* This theory is utilitarian, because the ultimate goal is to maximize the general welfare. However, the theory recognizes that we may use diverse strategies to pursue that goal. Sometimes we aim directly at it. For example, a senator may support a bill because she believes that it would raise the standard of living for everyone, or an individual may send money to the International Red Cross because he believes that this would do more good than any other action he might perform. But sometimes we don't think of the general welfare at all; instead, we simply care for our children, work at our jobs, obey the law, and keep our promises.

Right Action as Living According to the Best Plan. We can make the idea behind Multiple-Strategies Utilitarianism a little more specific.

Suppose we had a fully specified list of the virtues, motives, and methods of decision making that would enable a person to be happy and to contribute positively to the welfare of others. And suppose, further, that this is the *optimum* list for that person; there is no other combination of virtues, motives, and methods of decision making that would do a better job. The list would include at least the following:

- The virtues that are needed to make one's life go well
- The motives on which to act
- The commitments and personal relationships that one will have to friends, family, and others
- The social roles that one will occupy, with the responsibilities and demands that go with them
- The duties and concerns associated with the projects one will undertake, such as becoming a DJ or a soldier or an undertaker
- The everyday rules that one will usually follow without even thinking
- A strategy, or group of strategies, about when to consider making exceptions to the rules, and the grounds on which those exceptions can be made

The list would also specify the relations between the different items on the list—what takes priority over what, how to adjudicate conflicts, and so on. It would be very hard to construct such a list. As a practical matter, it might even be impossible.

But we can be fairly sure that it would include endorsements of friendship, honesty, and other familiar virtues. It would tell us to keep our promises, but not always, and to refrain from harming people, but not always; and so on. And it would probably tell us to stop living in luxury while each year millions of children die of preventable diseases.

At any rate, there is some combination of virtues, motives, and methods of decision making that is best *for me*, given my circumstances, personality, and talents—"best" in the sense that it will optimize the chances of my having a good life, while optimizing the chances of other people having good lives too. Call this optimum combination *my best plan*. The right thing for me to do is to act in accordance with my best plan.

My best plan may have a lot in common with yours. Presumably, they will both include rules against lying, stealing, and killing, together with an understanding about when to make exceptions to those rules. They will both include virtues such as patience, kindness, and self-control. They may both contain instructions for raising children, including what virtues to foster in them.

But our best plans need not be identical. People have different personalities and talents. One person may find fulfillment as a priest while another could never live like that. Thus, our lives might include different sorts of personal relationships, and we might need to cultivate different virtues. People also live in different circumstances and have access to different resources—some are rich; some are poor; some are privileged; some are persecuted. Thus, the optimum strategies for living will differ.

In each case, however, the identification of a plan as the best plan will be a matter of assessing how well it promotes the interests of everyone alike. So the overall theory is utilitarian, even though it may frequently endorse people acting from motives that do not look utilitarian at all.

13.5. The Moral Community

As moral agents, we should be concerned with everyone whose welfare might be affected by what we do. This may seem a pious platitude, but in reality it can be a hard doctrine. Every year, about a million children die of measles. Citizens in the affluent countries could easily cut this number in half, but they won't. People would no doubt do more if children in their own neighborhoods were dying, but the location of the children shouldn't matter: Everyone is included in the community of moral concern. If the interests of all children were taken seriously, wherever they lived, it would make a tremendous difference in our behavior.

If the moral community is not limited to people in one *place*, neither is it limited to people at any one *time*. Whether people will be affected by our actions now or in the future is irrelevant. Our obligation is to consider all their interests equally. One consequence of this pertains to nuclear weapons. Such weapons not only have the power to maim and kill innocent people, but they can also poison the environment for thousands of years. If the welfare of future generations is given proper weight, it is difficult to imagine any circumstance in which such weapons should be used. Climate change is another issue that affects the interests of future generations. If we fail to reverse the effects of global warming, our descendants will suffer even more than we will.

There is one other way in which our conception of the moral community must be expanded. Humans are not alone on this planet. Other sentient animals—that is, animals capable of feeling pleasure and pain—also have interests. When we abuse or kill them, they are harmed, just as humans are harmed when treated in those ways. Bentham and Mill were right to insist that the interests of nonhuman animals must be given weight in our moral calculations. As Bentham pointed out, excluding creatures from moral consideration because of their species is no more justified than excluding them because of their race, nationality, or sex. Impartiality requires the expansion of the moral community not only across space and time but across the boundaries of species as well. So, the single moral standard is not human welfare, but sentient welfare.

13.6. Justice and Fairness

Utilitarianism has been criticized as unfair and unjust. Can the complications we have introduced help?

One criticism has to do with punishment. We can imagine cases in which it promotes the general welfare to frame an innocent person. This is blatantly unjust, yet the Principle of Utility seems to endorse it. More generally, as Kant pointed out, the basic utilitarian "justification" of punishment is in terms of treating individuals as "mere means"—as tools for the advancement of society's goals, such as the reduction of future crime.

However, our theory takes a different view of punishment than utilitarians have usually taken. In fact, our view of punishment is close to Kant's. In punishing someone, we are treating him worse than we treat others. But this is justified, on our account, by the person's own past deeds. It is a response to what he has done. That is why it is not right to frame an innocent person; the innocent person has done nothing to deserve such treatment.

The theory of punishment, however, is only one aspect of justice. Questions of justice arise any time one person is treated differently from another. Suppose an employer must choose which of two employees to promote. The first candidate has worked hard, taking on extra work when needed, giving up vacation time to help out, and so on. The second candidate, on the other hand, has never done more than he had to. Obviously, the two employees will be treated very differently: One will get the promotion; the other will not. But this is all right, according to our theory. The first employee has earned the promotion; the second has not.

A person's voluntary actions can justify a departure from the policy of "equal treatment," but nothing else can. This goes against a common view of the matter. Often, people think it is right for individuals to be rewarded for physical beauty, superior intelligence, and other qualities that are due, in large part, to having the right DNA and the right parents. And in practice, people often have better jobs and more money just because they were born with greater natural gifts into wealthier families. But on reflection, this does not seem right. People do not deserve their native endowments; they have them only as a result of what John Rawls (1921–2002) calls "the natural lottery." Suppose the first employee in our example was passed over for the promotion, despite her hard work, because the second employee had some natural ability that was more useful in the new position. Even if the employer could justify this decision in terms of the company's needs, the first employee would rightly feel cheated. She has worked harder, yet he is getting the promotion, and the benefits that go with it, because of something he did nothing to earn. That is not fair. In a just society, people could improve their circumstances through hard work, but they would not benefit from a lucky birth.

13.7. Conclusion

What would a satisfactory moral theory look like? I have outlined the possibility that seems most plausible to me: According to Multiple-Strategies Utilitarianism, we should maximize the interests of all sentient beings by living according to our best plan. Modesty, however, is required when making such a proposal. Many great minds have devised such theories, and history has always found flaws in their conceptions. Still, there is reason for optimism, if not for my suggestion, then for some other proposal down the road. Civilization is only a few thousand years old. If we do not destroy ourselves, then the study of ethics has a bright future.

Notes on Sources

Chapter 1: What Is Morality?

The ethicists' comments about Baby Theresa are from an Associated Press report by David Briggs, "Baby Theresa Case Raises Ethics Questions," *The Champaign-Urbana News-Gazette*, March 31, 1992, p. A-6.

The poll about separating conjoined twins is from the *Ladies' Home Journal*, March 2001. The judges' comments about Jodie and Mary are from the *Daily Telegraph*, September 23, 2000.

Information about the Tracy Latimer case is from *The New York Times*, December 1, 1997, National Edition, p. A-3. The quotation is from the Canadian Broadcasting Corporation, January 19, 2001.

Chapter 2: The Challenge of Cultural Relativism

The story of the Greeks and the Callatians is from Herodotus, *The Histories*, translated by Aubrey de Selincourt, revised by A. R. Burn (Harmondsworth, Middlesex: Penguin Books, 1972), pp. 219–20. The quotation from Herodotus toward the end of the chapter is from the same source.

The information about the Eskimos is from Peter Freuchen, *Book of the Eskimos* (New York: Fawcett, 1961), and E. Adamson Hoebel, *The Law of Primitive Man* (Cambridge, MA: Harvard University Press, 1954), Chapter 5. The estimate of how female infanticide affects the male/female ratio in the Eskimo population is from Hoebel's work.

The William Graham Sumner quotation is from his *Folkways* (Boston: Ginn, 1906), p. 28.

The New York Times series on female genital mutilation included articles (mainly by Celia W. Dugger) published in 1996 on April 15, April 25, May 2, May 3, July 8, September 11, October 5, October 12, and December 28. I also learned about Fauziya Kassindja from her interview on PBS; see http://www.pbs.org/speaktruthtopower/fauziya.html. The figures of "28 African nations" and "about 120 million excisions" come from the World Health Organization's

"Eliminating Female Genital Mutilation: An Interagency Statement" (2008), pp. 7, 10, and Annex 3.

The story about the Saudi woman who was sentenced to being lashed comes from *The New York Times* (articles published on November 16 and December 18, 2007). The story about the Australian woman convicted on drug charges comes from a May 27, 2005, article in *The New York Times.* The story about the Nigerian woman sentenced to death comes from Associated Press articles on August 20, 2002, and September 25, 2003.

Chapter 3: Subjectivism in Ethics

The quotation from Matt Foreman is from *The New York Times,* June 25, 2001.

The Gallup Poll information is from www.gallup.com.

The Catholic view about homosexuality is quoted from *Catechism of the Catholic Church* (Mahwah, NJ: Paulist Press, 1994), p. 566.

The C. L. Stevenson quotation is from his *Ethics and Language* (New Haven, CT: Yale University Press, 1944), p. 114.

The story about Katie Shelton and Mark Friedrich is told on the Carnegie Hero Fund Commission's website: www.carnegiehero.org.

The quotation by James Dobson is from the April 2004 *Focus on the Family Newsletter,* which he read on the radio on March 24, 2004.

1,138 federal benefits tied to marriage: see the June 2005 "Harper's Index" in *Harper's Magazine* (source: U.S. General Accounting Office).

Chapter 4: Does Morality Depend on Religion?

77% of Americans support Judge Roy Moore: Gallup Poll, September 2003. 78% of Americans believe in God, and another 15% believe in a higher power: Gallup Poll, May 2008. I learned about the clergy's role in assigning movie ratings from the documentary *This Film Is Not Yet Rated* (2006).

The Bertrand Russell quotation is from his essay "A Free Man's Worship," in *Mysticism and Logic* (Garden City, NY: Doubleday, Anchor Books, n.d.), pp. 45–46.

Antony Flew makes the remark about philosophical talent in his *God and Philosophy* (New York: Dell, 1966), p. 109.

Hamlet's exact words were "Why, then 'tis none to you; for there is nothing either good or bad, but thinking makes it so: to me it is a prison" (Act 2, Scene 2, lines 254–56 of *The Tragedy of Hamlet, Prince of Denmark,* in *The Complete Works of William Shakespeare* [U.S.A.: Octopus Books, 1985, p. 844]).

The quotations from Aristotle are from *The Basic Works of Aristotle,* edited by Richard McKeon (New York: Random House, 1941), p. 249, and *The Politics,* translated by T. A. Sinclair (Harmondsworth, Middlesex: Penguin Books, 1962), p. 40.

The quotation from Saint Thomas Aquinas is from the *Summa Theologica,* III *Quodlibet,* 27, translated by Thomas Gilby in *St. Thomas Aquinas: Philosophical Texts* (New York: Oxford University Press, 1960).

The passage supposedly about abortion is Jeremiah 1:4–8. I quoted the "English Standard Version" translation of *The Holy Bible* (2001).

Chapter 5: Ethical Egoism

9.7 million children die each year from preventable causes, and 1.9 million from diarrhea: UNICEF's 2007 Annual Report, pp. 2 and 7.

For information about Raoul Wallenberg, see John Bierman, *The Righteous Gentile* (New York: Viking Press, 1981). For information about Gentiles who risked their lives to protect Jews, see www.yadvashem.org.

The information about Zell Kravinsky comes from "The Gift," an article by Ian Parker in *The New Yorker* (August 2, 2004). The information about Oseola McCarty comes from Bill Clinton, *Giving: How Each of Us Can Change the World* (New York: Alfred A. Knopf, 2007), p. 26.

The story about Abraham Lincoln is from the Springfield *Monitor,* quoted by Frank Sharp in his *Ethics* (New York: Appleton Century, 1928), p. 75.

The story about the man who leapt onto the train tracks is from the January 3, 2007, edition of *The New York Times.*

The quotations from Ayn Rand are from her book *The Virtue of Selfishness* (New York: Signet, 1964), pp. 27, 32, 80, and 81.

The newspaper stories are from the *Baltimore Sun,* August 28, 2001; *The Miami Herald,* August 28, 1993, October 6, 1994, and June 2, 1989; *The New York Times,* April 28, 2008; and the *Macon Telegraph,* July 15, 2005.

For Kurt Baier's argument, see his book *The Moral Point of View* (Ithaca, NY: Cornell University Press, 1958), pp. 189–90.

Chapter 6: The Idea of a Social Contract

Hobbes's estimate of the state of nature is from his *Leviathan,* Oake-shott edition (Oxford: Blackwell, 1960), Chapter 13. See p. 82.

The Rousseau quotation is from *The Social Contract and Discourses,* translated by G. D. H. Cole (New York: Dutton, 1959), pp. 18–19.

That Flood and Dresher first formulated the Prisoner's Dilemma around 1950 is mentioned in Richmond Campbell, "Background for the Uninitiated," *Paradoxes of Rationality and Cooperation,* edited by Richmond Campbell and Lanning Sowden (Vancouver: University of British Columbia Press, 1985), p. 3.

The quotations from King and Waldman may be found in *Civil Disobedience: Theory and Practice,* edited by Hugo Adam Bedau (New York: Pegasus Books, 1967), pp. 76–77, 78, 106, and 107.

The Hume quotation is from "Of the Original Contract," reprinted in *Hume's Moral and Political Philosophy,* edited by Henry D. Aiken (New York: Hafner Publishing Company, 1948), p. 363.

Chapter 7: The Utilitarian Approach

The quotations from Bentham are from his book *The Principles of Morals and Legislation,* p. 125 (on God) and p. 311 (on animals), available in many reprintings.

The account of Freud's death was taken from Ronald W. Clark, *Freud: The Man and the Cause* (New York: Random House, 1980), pp. 525–527, and Paul Ferris, *Dr. Freud: A Life* (Washington, DC: Counterpoint, 1997), pp. 395–397.

The quotation from Mill's *On Liberty* (1859) is from paragraph 8 of Chapter 1, "Introductory."

Bentham discusses sexual ethics in "Offences Against One's Self," written around 1785 and published posthumously.

Most of the information on marijuana comes from *Pot Politics: Marijuana and the Costs of Prohibition,* edited by Mitch Earleywine (Oxford University Press, 2007). The essays cited below are from that book.

From Mitch Earleywine, "Thinking Clearly About Marijuana Policy," pp. 3–16: One-third of Americans have tried pot (p. 4); on the Gateway Theory (pp. 7–8); when crack is more widely available (p. 8); the William Bennett quotation (p. 9); marijuana does not cause violence (p. 10).

From Kevin A. Sabet, "The (Often Unheard) Case Against Marijuana Leniency," pp. 325–352: One joint is like six cigarettes (p. 328, citing the British Lung Foundation from 2002).

From Wayne Hall, "A Cautious Case for Cannabis Depenalization," pp. 91–112: on driving (p. 92); on the respiratory system (pp. 92–93); on cognitive damage (p. 95); on the Gateway Theory (pp. 96–97); on the difficulties ex-cons face finding jobs (p. 102).

From Daniel Egan and Jeffrey A. Miron, "The Budgetary Implications of Marijuana Prohibition," pp. 17–39: on enforcement costs and possible tax gains (p. 29).

From Robert Gore and Mitch Earleywine, "Marijuana's Perceived Addictiveness: A Survey of Clinicians and Researchers," pp. 176–186: Pot is less addictive than caffeine (p. 179). Gore and Earleywine surveyed 746 drug abuse counselors, mental health specialists, and academic researchers.

From Anthony Liguori, "Marijuana and Driving: Trends, Design Issues, and Future Recommendations," pp. 71–90: See especially p. 83.

In 2007, 5.8% of Americans aged 12 and older had used pot in the past month: "Results from the 2007 National Survey on Drug Use and Health: National Findings," p. 1.

Americans spend more than $10 billion per year on marijuana: the Office of National Drug Control Policy's *2008 Marijuana Sourcebook* gives only the old figure that Americans spent $10.5 billion in 2000 (p. 11).

In 2007, there were around 872,720 marijuana arrests: *Crime in the United States, 2007* (Department of Justice/Federal Bureau of Investigation), combining information from the "Persons Arrested" page (http://www.fbi.gov/ucr/cius2007/arrests/index.html) and "Table 29" (http://www.fbi.gov/ucr/cius2007/data/table_29.html). The 44,000+ figure is based on the government's reporting of the number of drug offenders in prison and the percentage of such offenders serving time for marijuana crimes.

The quotations from Aquinas about animals are from *Summa Contra Gentiles*, Book 3, Chapter 112. See *Basic Writings of St. Thomas Aquinas*, edited by Anton C. Pegis, (New York: Random House, 1945), Vol. 2, p. 222.

Peter Singer says that morality is not a system of nasty puritanical prohibitions in *Practical Ethics*, 2nd ed. (Cambridge University Press, 1993), p. 1.

Richard D. Ryder, "Speciesism in the Laboratory," *In Defense of Animals: The Second Wave*, edited by Peter Singer (Oxford: Blackwell, 2006). Ryder coined "speciesism": p. ix; the experiments: pp. 91–92.

Chapter 8: The Debate over Utilitarianism

McCloskey's example of the utilitarian tempted to bear false witness is from his paper "A Non-Utilitarian Approach to Punishment," *Inquiry* 8 (1965), pp. 239–55.

G. E. Moore discusses what has intrinsic value in the last chapter of *Principia Ethica* (Cambridge University Press, 1903).

The quotation from Mill about impartiality is in chapter 2 of his *Utilitarianism* (1861; available in various reprintings).

The quotation from John Cottingham is from his article "Partialism, Favouritism and Morality," *Philosophical Quarterly* 36 (1986), p. 357.

The Smart quotation is from J. J. C. Smart and Bernard Williams, *Utilitarianism: For and Against* (Cambridge University Press, 1973), p. 68. "Rule worship" is discussed on p. 10.

Frances Howard-Snyder, "Rule Consequentialism Is a Rubber Duck," *American Philosophical Quarterly* 30 (1993), pp. 271–278.

See Gunnar Myrdal, *An American Dilemma: The Negro Problem and American Democracy* (1944; available in various reprintings).

Chapter 9: Are There Absolute Moral Rules?

The quotation from Franklin Roosevelt is from his communication *The President of the United States to the Governments of France, Germany, Italy, Poland and His Britannic Majesty,* September 1, 1939.

The excerpts from Truman's diary are from Robert H. Ferrell, *Off the Record: The Private Papers of Harry S. Truman* (New York: Harper & Row, 1980), pp. 55–56.

The Churchill quote is from Winston S. Churchill, *The Second World War, Volume VI: Triumph and Tragedy* (New York: Houghton Mifflin Company, 1953), p. 553.

Anscombe's 1939 pamphlet "The Justice of the Present War Examined," as well as her 1956 pamphlet "Mr. Truman's Degree," can be found in G. E. M. Anscombe, *Ethics, Religion and Politics: Collected Philosophical Papers,* Vol. III (Minneapolis: University of Minnesota Press, 1981). See pp. 34, 64, and 65.

The grisly details about Hiroshima are from Richard Rhodes, *The Making of the Atomic Bomb* (New York: Simon & Schuster, 1986), p. 715 (birds igniting in midair) and pp. 725–26 (people dying in water).

Kant's statement of the Categorical Imperative is from his *Foundations of the Metaphysics of Morals,* translated by Lewis White Beck (Indianapolis, IN: Bobbs-Merrill, 1959), p. 39.

Anscombe's criticism of Kant is from "Modern Moral Philosophy," *Philosophy*, Vol. 33, No. 124 (January 1958), pp. 1–19, reprinted in *Ethics, Religion and Politics: The Collected Philosophical Papers of G. E. M. Anscombe*, Vol. III (Minneapolis: University of Minnesota Press, 1981).

Kant's "On a Supposed Right to Lie from Altruistic Motives" can be found in *Critique of Practical Reason and Other Writings in Moral Philosophy*, translated by Lewis White Beck (University of Chicago Press, 1949). The quotation is from p. 348.

The Peter Geach quotation is from his *God and the Soul* (London: Routledge & Kegan Paul, 1969), p. 128.

MacIntyre's remark is at the beginning of the chapter on Kant in his *A Short History of Ethics* (New York: Macmillan, 1966).

Chapter 10: Kant and Respect for Persons

Kant's remarks on animals are from his *Lectures on Ethics,* translated by Louis Infield (New York: Harper & Row, 1963), pp. 239–40. I altered one sentence without changing its meaning: "he who is cruel to animals also becomes hard in his dealings with men" (not "becomes hard also").

The second formulation of the Categorical Imperative, in terms of treating persons as ends, is in *Foundations of the Metaphysics of Morals*, translated by Lewis White Beck (Indianapolis, IN: Bobbs-Merrill, 1959), p. 47. The remarks about "dignity" and "price" are on p. 53.

Bentham's statement "All punishment is mischief" is from *The Principles of Morals and Legislation* (New York: Hafner, 1948), p. 170.

The quotations from Kant on punishment are from *The Metaphysical Elements of Justice,* translated by John Ladd (Indianapolis, IN: Bobbs-Merrill, 1965), pp. 99–107, except for the quotation about the "right good beating," which is from *Critique of Practical Reason,* translated by Lewis White Beck (University of Chicago Press, 1949), p. 170.

On the change in terminology from "prisons" to "correctional facilities," see Blake McKelvey, *American Prisons: A History of Good Intentions* (Montclair, NJ: Patterson Smith, 1977), p. 357.

The prison statistics come from the Pew Center on the States' report, "One in 100: Behind Bars in America 2008," and are confirmed by the U.S. Department of Justice website. On changes in the American prison system between the 1960s and 1990s, see Eric Schlosser, "The Prison-Industrial Complex," the *Atlantic Monthly*, Vol. 282, No. 6 (December 1998).

On December 22, 2006, a story on *National Public Radio* cited California officials as saying that California has the highest recidivism rate in the country.

Jesus talks about "turning the other cheek" in Matthew 5:38–39. I have used the "English Standard Version" translation of *The Holy Bible* (2001).

Chapter 11: Feminism and the Ethics of Care

Heinz's Dilemma is explained in Lawrence Kohlberg, *Essays on Moral Development*, Vol. 1: *The Philosophy of Moral Development* (New York: Harper & Row, 1981), p. 12. For the six stages of moral development, see the same work, pp. 409–12.

Amy and Jake are quoted by Carol Gilligan in her *In a Different Voice: Psychological Theory and Women's Development* (Cambridge, MA: Harvard University Press, 1982), pp. 26, 28. The other quotations from Gilligan are from pp. 16–17, 31.

The Virginia Held quotation is from her "Feminist Transformations of Moral Theory," *Philosophy and Phenomenological Research* 50 (1990), p. 344.

Women score higher than men on empathy tests: M. H. Davis, "Measuring Individual Differences in Empathy: Evidence for a Multidimensional Approach," *Journal of Personality and Social Psychology*, Vol. 44, No. 1 (January 1983), pp. 113–126 and P. E. Jose, "The Role of Gender and Gender Role Similarity in Readers' Identification with Story Characters," *Sex Roles*, Vol. 21, Nos. 9–10 (November 1989), pp. 697–713.

Brain scans and punishment: Tania Singer et al., "Empathetic neural Responses Are Modulated by the Perceived Fairness of Others," *Nature*, Vol. 439 (January 26, 2006), pp. 466–469.

Roy F. Baumeister, "Is There Anything Good About Men?" American Psychological Association, Invited Address, 2007 (quotation from p. 9).

Women are only slightly more care-oriented than men: Sara Jaffee and Janet Shibley Hyde, "Gender Differences in Moral Orientation: A Meta-Analysis," *Psychological Bulletin*, Vol. 126, No. 5 (2000), pp. 703–726.

Male/female differences appear at early age: Larry Cahill, "His Brain, Her Brain," *Scientific American*, April 25, 2005 (8 pages), citing the work of Simon Baron-Cohen and Svetlana Lutchmaya.

"'Care' is the new buzzword": Annette Baier, *Moral Prejudices* (Cambridge, MA: Harvard University Press, 1994), p. 19. The other quotations from Baier are from p. 4 ("connect their ethics of love") and p. 2 ("honorary women").

The figures about HIV are from UNICEF's 2007 Annual Report, p. 9.

The quotations from Nel Noddings are from her book *Caring: A Feminine Approach to Ethics and Moral Education* (Berkeley: University of California Press, 1984), pp. 149–55.

Chapter 12: The Ethics of Virtue

Elizabeth Anscombe proposes to jettison the notion of "morally right" in her article "Modern Moral Philosophy," *Philosophy* 33 (1958), pp. 1–19, reprinted in *Ethics, Religion and Politics: The Collected Philosophical Papers of G. E. M. Anscombe*, Vol. III (Minneapolis: University of Minnesota Press, 1981). The quotation at the beginning of the chapter actually picks up in the middle of one of Anscombe's sentences, and several pages separate the two parts of the quote.

The quotations from Aristotle are from Book II of the *Nicomachean Ethics*, translated by Martin Ostwald (Indianapolis, IN: Bobbs-Merrill, 1962), except for the quotation about friendship, which is from Book VIII, and the quotation about visiting foreign lands, which is Martha C. Nussbaum's translation in her article "Non-Relative Virtues: An Aristotelian Approach," in *Midwest Studies in Philosophy*, Vol. XIII: *Ethical Theory: Character and Virtue*, edited by Peter A. French, Theodore E. Uehling, Jr., and Howard K. Wettstein (Notre Dame, IN: University of Notre Dame Press, 1988), pp. 32–53.

Pincoffs's suggestion about the nature of virtue appears in his book *Quandaries and Virtues: Against Reductivism in Ethics* (Lawrence: University of Kansas Press, 1986), p. 78.

Peter Geach's remark about courage is from his book *The Virtues* (Cambridge University Press, 1977), p. xxx. The story about Saint Athanasius appears on p. 114.

Jesus says that we should give all we have to help the poor in Matthew 19:21–24; Mark 10:21–25; and Luke 18:22–25.

Plato's *Euthyphro* is available in several translations, including Hugh Tredennick and Harold Tarrant's in *Plato: The Last Days of Socrates* (New York: Penguin Books, 2003).

The Nietzsche quotation is from *Twilight of the Idols*, "Morality as Anti-Nature," Part 6, translated by Walter Kaufmann in *The Portable Nietzsche* (New York: Viking Press, 1954), p. 491.

Michael Stocker's example is from his article "The Schizophrenia of Modern Ethical Theories," *Journal of Philosophy* 73 (1976), pp. 453–66.

The John Stuart Mill quotation is from Chapter 2 of his *Utilitarianism* (1861; Available in various reprintings).

Chapter 13: What Would a Satisfactory Moral Theory Be Like?

The age of the universe is taken from the "WMAP" data as presented on NASA's website in 2008. "WMAP" is the Wilkinson Microwave Anisotropy Probe, which was launched in 2001 and is still collecting information.

The Sidgwick quotation is from Henry Sidgwick, *The Methods of Ethics,* 7th ed. (London: Macmillan, 1907), p. 413.

John Rawls discusses the "natural lottery" on p. 74 of *A Theory of Justice* (Cambridge, Mass.: Harvard University Press, 1971) and on p. 64 of the revised edition of that book, published in 1999.

Index

Abortion, 41
  Bible and, 59–60
  history of opinions on, 60–61
  humanity of fetus and, 58–59
  religion and, 58–61
ACLU. *See* American Civil
  Liberties Union
Act-Utilitarianism, 122
Agents. *See* Moral agents
Altruism. *See also* Ethical Egoism
  alleged, 67
  limited, 81
  as possible, 64–65
  Rand on ethics of, 71–72
  as self-defeating, 70–71
American Civil Liberties Union
  (ACLU), 49–50
American Prison Association, 141
Anencephaly, 1–2

Animals
  experiments, 107–8
  nonhuman, 104–8
  obligations to nonhuman,
    154–55
Anscombe, Elizabeth, 124–27
  on lying, 130
  on modern moral philosophy,
    159–60
Aquinas, Thomas, 60, 104
Argument(s). *See also*
  Disagreements
  assessing, 11–12
  bad v. good, 11
  Benefits, 3
  conjoined twins and, 6
  Cultural Differences, 17–19
  Ethical Egoism, 69–79
  forms of, 17

against homosexuality, 44–47
    invalid, 18
    on organ transplant, 3
    from sanctity of life, 7
    for saving as many as can, 6
    Slippery Slope, 9–10, 12
    as sound, 18
    from wrongness of
        discriminating against
        handicapped, 8–9
    from wrongness of
        killing, 4–5
Aristotle, 53–54, 158
    on women, 146
Artifacts, 54
Attitude
    of care, 155
    disagreements in, 38
Autonomy, 4

Baby Theresa. *See* Pearson,
        Theresa Ann Campo
Baier, Kurt, 75–76
Baumeister, Roy, 150
Beliefs
    about morals, 27
    of different societies, 18
Beneficence, 55, 71
Bennett, William, 101
Bentham, Jeremy, 105–6
    morality, 97–98
    on punishment, 139
Bible
    abortion and, 59–60
    on homosexuality, 46–47
Big bang, 173–74
Bill and Melinda Gates
        Foundation, 65
Brain, death, 5

Bush, George H. W., 101

Callatians, 14–15, 18–19
Care
    attitude of, 155
    ethics of, 146–57, 154
Categorical Imperative, 127
    Kant on, 128–29, 137–39
    rejection of, 133–34
Cerebral palsy, 7–8
Character, 158
Children, 153–54. *See also*
        Handicapped children
China, 19
Christianity, 50. *See also* Bible
    on abortion, 59–60
    on homosexuality, 46–47
    human life in, 99
    nonhuman animals in, 104
Circumcision, female, 24–26
Civil disobedience
    examples of, 90
    problem of, 90–92
Common sense, 63, 122–23
    as wrong, 120
Communication, 23
Communities, 163–64
    moral, 180–81
Conjoined twins, 5
    argument for saving as many
        as can and, 6
    operations on, 6
Consequences
    good, 117
    in Utilitarianism, 111–14,
        117–18
Cottingham, John, 116
Courage, 161
Creation, 136

Criminal punishment, Kant
  and, 139–45
Criminals, 144–45
Crisis, reaction to, 63
The Critique of Practical Reason
  (Kant), 139–40
Cultural Relativism
  appeal of, 31
  challenge of, 14–31
  claims of, 27–29
  essence of, 19
  implications of, 20
  learning from, 29–31
  observation of, 16–17
  tolerance and, 17
  as true, 19–21
Cultures
  criticism of, 26
  Eskimo, 15, 17–18, 21–22
  gender in Eskimo, 21–22
  judging, 16
  moral codes of different,
    14–16, 27
  norms of, 17
  undesirable practices of,
    24–26
  values shared by all, 23–24
Customs, 19
  criticizing, 26
  of Eskimos, 15

Darwin, Charles, 151
Death
  brain, 5
  changing conception of, 5
  penalty, 143–44
Debate, 109–23
Desire, 66, 137
Development, moral, 147–52

Dignity, 136–37
Disagreements
  in attitude, 38
  Emotivism and, 37–38
Discrimination, against
  handicapped, 8–9
Disobedience. *See* Civil
  disobedience
Divine Command Theory,
  50–53
Dobson, James, 45–46
Dresher, Melvin, 83
Dress, modesty of, 30
Drugs. *See* Marijuana
Duty, 62, 136, 153
  harm and, 73–74
  impersonal, 156
  lying and, 74
  to others, 63
  promise and, 74
  voice of, 83

Egoism. *See* Ethical Egoism;
  Psychological Egoism
Emotivism
  disagreement and, 37–38
  as flawed, 40–41
  language and, 26
  moral judgments and, 38–39
Eskimos
  customs of, 15
  gender in culture of, 21–22
  infanticide in culture of, 15,
    17–18, 21
Ethical Egoism, 62–68, 159
  arguments against, 74–79
  arguments for, 69–74
  commonsense morality
    compatibility of, 73–74

as logically inconsistent,
    75–76
metaphysical basis for, 72
self-interest and, 69–70
as unacceptably arbitrary,
    77–79
wicked action and, 74–75
Ethical Subjectivism
    attraction of, 41
    basic idea of, 32–33
    evolution of theory of, 33–34
Ethics. *See also* Natural Law
    Theory
    of care, 146–57, 153
    proofs in, 41–44
    reason's role in, 39–41,
        174–75
    revolution in, 97–98
    of right action, 158–60
    skepticism about, 16
    subjectivism in, 32–47
    of virtue, 156–72
Ethics and Language
    (Stevenson), 40
Euthanasia, 98–101
Euthyphro (Plato), 165
Evolution, 151, 173–74
Excision, 24
    effects of, 25
Experiments, on animals, 107–8

Fairness, 181–83
Falwell, Jerry, 32–35
Family values, 44–46
Feelings
    moral reasoning and, 10
    truth and, 11
Feminism, ethics of care and,
    146–57
Flew, Antony, 51

Flood, Merrill M., 83
Foreman, Matt, 32, 34–35
*Foundations of the Metaphysics of
    Morals* (Kant), 128–29
Freud, Sigmund, 98–99, 99–100
Friendship, 164
Funerary practices, 29

Gandhi, Mohandas K., 90–92
Gay men. *See* Homosexuality
Gay rights, 32–33
Geach, Anscombe, 127, 132
Geach, Peter, 162, 163
Gender, in Eskimo culture,
    21–22
Generosity, 162
Geography, 18
Greeks, 14, 18–19

Handicapped, discriminating
    against, 8–9
Handicapped children
    Baby Theresa, 1–5
    Jodie and Mary, 5–6
    Tracy Latimer, 7–10
Happiness
    morality and, 97–98
    in Utilitarianism, 98–101
    as valued, 26
Health, 62. *See also* World Health
    Organization
Hedonism, 110–11
Herodotus, 30–31
HIV, children with, 153–54
Hobbes, Thomas
    on morality, 80–84
    on social contract, 82–83
    on state of nature, 80–82
Homosexuality, 32–33

Bible on, 46–47
dispute about, 44–47
expression of, 44
"family values" argument
    against, 44–46
"unnaturalness" argument
    against, 44–47
Honesty, 163. *See also* Lying
Humanity, 58–59
Hume, David, 41, 56, 94–95

Impartiality
    ideal of, 169
    moral reasoning and, 12–13
    requirements of, 12–13
Implications
    of Cultural Relativism, 20
    for moral judgments, 152–55
Incompleteness, problem of,
    170–72
Infanticide, 15, 17–18, 21
Insight, of Kant, 133–35
IVF, 10

Jodie and Mary, conjoined
    twins, 5–6
Judaism, 50
Judgments. *See* Moral judgments
Justice, 111–12
    Utilitarianism and, 182–83

Kant, Immanuel, 159
    on Categorical Imperative,
        128–29, 137–38
    on consistency, 134
    core ideas of, 136–39
    criminal punishment and,
        139–45

insight of, 133–35
on lying, 127–28, 129–32
respect for persons and,
    136–45
on Retributivism, 141–45
Kassindja, Fauziya, 24–25
Killing
    argument from wrongness
        of, 4–5
    mercy, 10, 100
    morality of, 99
    in self-defense, 5
    types of, 99
    as wrong, 8–9
King, Martin Luther, Jr., civil
    disobedience and, 90–92
Knowledge, moral, 56–57
Kohlberg, Lawrence, moral
    development stages of,
    147–50
Kravinsky, Zell, 65, 67–68

Ladies Home Journal, 6
Language
    Emotivism and, 36
    moral, 37, 40
Latimer, Tracy, 7–10
Laws. *See also* Natural Law
    Theory
    obeying, 92
Lectures on Ethics (Kant), 136
Lesbian women. *See*
    Homosexuality
Leviathan (Hobbes), 81
Life, sanctity of human, 7
Lincoln, Abraham, 67–68
Loyalty, 164–65
Luxuries, 62–63
Lying, 42–43, 121
    Anscombe on, 130

duty and, 74
Kant on, 127–28, 129–32

MacIntyre, Alasdair, 133
Malnutrition, health problems
    from, 62
Marijuana
    costs associated with, 103–4
    disadvantages of, 102–3
    morality and, 101–2
    utilitarian view of, 101–4
Marriage, monogamous, 29–30
McCarty, Oseola, 65
McCloskey, H. J., 111–12, 121–22
Mercy killing, 10, 100
Mill, James, 97
Mill, John Stuart, 97–98,
        109–10, 169
    on moral agents, 152–53
Montgomery Bus Boycott, 90
Moore, G. E., 111
Moore, Roy, 48–49
Moral agents, conscientious, 13
Moral codes
    of different cultures,
        14–16, 27
    societies', 16–17, 19–20
    standards and, 16
Moral community, 180
    time/place of, 181
Moral judgments, 10
    Emotivism and, 38–39
    good reasons backing, 134
    implications for, 152–55
    moral reasoning and, 11–12
    personal tastes v., 11
    proofs of, 42
    as supported, 43
Moral law, 159
Moral philosophy, defined, 1

The Moral Point of View (Baier),
        75–76
Moral principles, 12, 52
Moral progress, 20
Moral reasoning
    feelings and, 10
    impartiality and, 12–13
    moral judgments and, 11–12
Moral rules, 23–24, 87–88
    absolute, 124–35
Moral standards, 178
Moral theory, satisfactory,
        173–83
Moral truths, 41, 57
    objectivity/universality of, 16
Morality
    as acting on reason, 174–75
    Bentham on, 97–98
    defining, 1–13
    demands of, 88–89
    drawing conclusions about, 17
    Ethical Egoism as compatible
        with commonsense, 73–74
    happiness and, 97–98
    Hobbes on, 80–84
    without hubris, 173–75
    as independent matter, 61
    of killing, 99
    marijuana and, 101–2
    minimum conception
        of, 1, 13
    mysterious conception of, 51
    Principle of Utility and, 98
    Prisoner's Dilemma and,
        85–87
    religion and, 48–61
    requirements of, 10
    rules of, 95
Morals, beliefs about, 27
Motivation, 168–69
Motives, 67–68, 176–77

Multiple-Strategies
    Utilitarianism, 177–80, 183
Myrdal, Gunnar, 123

Natural Law Theory, 53–57
Nazis, 17, 64–65
Need, equality of, 81
Nicomachean Ethics (Aristotle), 158
Nietzsche, Friedrich, 166–67
Noddings, Nel, 154

Obama, Barack, 40
Obligations, 128, 154
    to nonhuman animals, 154–55
    theories of, 152
Operations, on conjoined twins, 6
Organ transplant
    Benefits Argument around, 3
    moral dilemma around, 2
    Pearson and, 2–5
    people used as means and, 3–4

Parks, Rosa, 90
Pearson, Theresa Ann Campo, 1–2
    organ transplant and, 2–5
Pincoffs, Edmund L., 160
Plans, best, 179–80
Plato, 165
Pleasure
    as ultimate good, 110
    in Utilitarianism, 109–11
Polyamory, 30
Prejudice, 11–12, 40
Principle of Equal Treatment,
    77–79
Principle of Utility, 182
    as guide for choosing rules,
    118–20

morality and, 98
    trusting, 121
Principles, moral, 12
Prisoner's Dilemma, 83–87
Progress, moral, 20
Proofs, in ethics, 41–44
Psychological Egoism, 63–69
    as false, 175
Punishment. *See also* Criminal
        punishment
    Bentham on, 139
    capital, 143–44
    justifications of, 182
    as proportional to crime, 142
    retribution/utility in theory
        of, 139–45
    theory of, 182
    utilitarian view of, 141

Racism, 78–79, 175
Rand, Ayn, 73
    on ethics of altruism, 71–72
Rawls, John, on natural
        lottery, 182
Reasoning. *See also* Moral
        reasoning
    ethics and, 39–41, 174–75
    morality and, 174–75
    requirements of, 175
Reform, social, 20
Rejection, of Categorical
        Imperative, 133–34
Relationships, 116
Relativism. *See* Cultural Relativism
Religion. *See also* Christianity
    abortion and, 58–61
    in America, 49
    Divine Command Theory,
        50–53
    moral issues and, 57–61

morality and, 48–61
Theory of Natural Law, 53–57
Respect, Kant and, 136–45
Retribution, punishment and,
    139–45
Retributivism
    Kant on, 141–45
    power of, 145
Rights, 112–13. *See also* Gay rights
    in Utilitarianism, 113–14
Roosevelt, Franklin D., 124
Rousseau, Jean-Jacques, 82–83
Rules. *See also* Moral rules
    breaking moral, 88
    conflicts between, 132–33
    of morality, 95
    Principle of Utility as guide
        for choosing, 118–20
    as valid, 94–95
    worship, 119
Rule-Utilitarianism, 118–19
Russell, Bertrand, 49–50
Ryder, Richard D., 106

Satisfaction, 66–67
Scarcity, 81
Schur, Max, 99
Science, 56
Scriptures, 57–61
Self-defense, killing in, 5
Self-interest, 63–64, 80–81
    pursuing, 69–70
Seriousness, moral, 10
Sexual behavior, 100–101. *See
    also* Homosexuality
    promiscuous, 87
    purpose of, 45
    "unnatural," 44–47
Sidgwick, Henry, 178
Slippery Slope Argument,
    9–10, 12

Smart, J. J. C., 119–20
Social Contract Theory, 159
    advantages to, 87–89
    difficulties for, 93–96
    idea of, 80–86
The Social Contract (Rousseau),
    82–83
Societies
    beliefs of, 18
    moral codes of, 16–17,
        19–20, 27
    values of, 21
    virtues in different, 167
Socrates, 1, 51
Speciesism, 106
Standards
    moral, 178
    moral codes and, 16
State of nature, 80–82
    escaping, 82
Stevenson, Charles L., 36, 40
Stocker, Michael, 168
Subjectivism. *See also* Ethical
        Subjectivism
    in ethics, 32–47
    Simple, 34–36
Sumner, William Graham
    on essence of Cultural
        Relativism, 19
    on right way, 16

Ten Commandments, 48–49
Theories. *See* Divine Command
        Theory; Moral theory;
        Natural Law Theory; Social
        Contract Theory; Virtue
        Theory
Tolerance, of cultural
        relativists, 17
Treatment. *See also* Principle of
        Equal Treatment

as deserved, 175–76
of women, 27–28
Truman, Harry S., 124–27,
131, 135
Truth. *See also* Moral truths
feelings and, 11
objective, 18
Truth telling. *See* Lying
Twins. *See* Conjoined twins

UNICEF, 153–54
Utilitarianism, 159
Act-, 122
backward-looking reasons
and, 114
classical, 109
consequences in, 111–14,
117–18
criticisms of, 182–83
debate over, 109–23
defense of, 116–22
as demanding, 115–16, 122
happiness in, 98–101
marijuana and, 101–4
morality in, 98
motive, 178
Multiple-Strategies, 177–80,
179, 183
nonhuman animals and, 105–8
personal relationships and, 116
pleasure in, 109–11
practical applications of, 98
punishment and, 141
rights in, 113–14
Rule-, 118–19
as unfair, 182–83
as unjust, 182–83
values and, 120–21
Utility. *See also* Principle
of Utility

punishment in theory of,
139–45

Values, 21
family, 44–46
of object, 137
universal, 23–24
utilitarian basis of, 120–21
Vanity, 69
Virtue(s)
conduct and, 169–70
as defined, 160–61
Divine Law and, 158
ethics of, 156–72
for everyone, 166–68
features of distinct, 161–65
importance of, 165–66
moral, 161
radical ethics of, 171–72
society and, 167
Virtue Theory, 156–57, 172
advantages of, 168–69
Anscombe on, 159–60
components of, 160–68
moral motivation and, 168–69

Waldman, Louis, 91–92
Wallenberg, Raoul, 64–65
War, 82
Women
Aristotle, 146
discrimination against, 146
mistreatment of, 27–28
social roles of, 151
World Health Organization, 24

York v. Story, 112–13